DRAWN by
GOD

DRAWN by GOD

THE MEETING - THE DATING - THE MARRIAGE

DIANE WILSON

Outskirts Press, Inc.
Denver, Colorado

The opinions expressed in this manuscript are solely the opinions of the author and do not represent the opinions or thoughts of the publisher. The author has represented and warranted full ownership and/or legal right to publish all the materials in this book.

Drawn By God
The Meeting, The Dating, The Marriage
All Rights Reserved.
Copyright © 2012 Diane Wilson
v4.0

Cover design by: Maurice Jones, Majonesinc.com

This book may not be reproduced, transmitted, or stored in whole or in part by any means, including graphic, electronic, or mechanical without the express written consent of the publisher except in the case of brief quotations embodied in critical articles and reviews.

Outskirts Press, Inc.
http://www.outskirtspress.com

ISBN: 978-1-4327-7196-6

Outskirts Press and the "OP" logo are trademarks belonging to Outskirts Press, Inc.

PRINTED IN THE UNITED STATES OF AMERICA

Table of Contents

Introduction vii
Dedication ix
About the Author xi
Foreword xiii
Chapter 1:   The Meeting 1
Chapter 2:   Intimacy with God 19
Chapter 3:   The Awe of God 27
Chapter 4:   Drawn by God 33
Chapter 5:   Dating God 41
Chapter 6:   The Marriage 45
Chapter 7:   Broken Vows 51
Chapter 8:   The Divorce 67
Chapter 9:   Being Reconciled to God 71

Introduction

Drawn by God is a breathtaking, eye catching story based on truth and true life experiences. It will take you down different avenues, into the night and lightest of days. It will lead you into the throne room of glory, across plains and through the depths of an ocean by way of your imagination. It will leave you with a greater appreciation of who God is and have you wanting more of Him. Drawn by God is guaranteed to draw you closer to God with a heart of repentance and a mind stayed on Him.

Dedication

*Lord, as I dedicate this book to you, continue to draw me. This book is dedicated to my daughter Qiana; I love you so much, **never** leave the "Ark of Safety." To my father Willie Lee Wilson Sr., you gave me a story to tell. To my pastor and author of several excellent books, Dr. Bishop Jimmie A. Ellis III, you are one of the most amazing teacher on earth. Thank you for helping me to take territory. To my best friend Edwina E. Hawthorne, woman of God you never cease to amaze me. To Pastor Benjamin Green, a million thanks to you. You are a wonderful friend. To everyone who encouraged and supported me, thank you.*

About the Author

Diane Wilson has been writing since her early teenage years. Writing poetry was and still is a hobby for her. In high school encouraged by an English teacher to write, she's written several plays and hopes to one day write a script. Drawn by God has taken Diane to a higher level of writing. Drawn by God is full of personal truth, bringing back memories from the days of old to times of the present. An avid reader with several books to follow, Diane will keep you anxiously awaiting her next soon to be released novel. Never separated from her pen or pad, as she writes, the pages come to life painting pictures never seen.

Foreword

I found this book to be easy reading, non technical, however, profoundly relative to the believer's evolution and maturation in God. Written in the flow of a good novel, yet autobiographically true, and at times convicting with provocations for greater intimacy with the Lord. I enjoyed the snippets of the author's life, experiences and analogies. The compilation of chapters is sound in the Word and is therefore applicable for all believers, regardless of the number of years they may have amassed in Christ. I recommend reading this book and keeping it as part of your collection......for frequent reading!

Pastor Benjamin Green
Abiding Truth Ministries

1
The Meeting

How do we meet God and what happens when we do? From time to time I often thought about how people came to know Jesus Christ as their Lord and Savior. How did they meet Him? Who played a part in their receiving salvation? Was it a crisis that drew them to God? Was it fear or the loss of a very close loved one so dear that God was the only answer? Did their parents make them go to church like mine did? Was it the words from a tract or a book? Did they hit rock bottom or did the voice of God ring in their ears so loud that it shook the very core of their soul? I pondered these and other questions while growing up and walking in my salvation. I've heard some of the answers to these questions from people who had the opportunity to tell them. Some of them were sad and some of them were happy stories. The end result was that they met their God. Everyone who has had an encounter with God in one way or another has a story to tell but no one can tell your story like you can. This is my story.

I was told about God at a very early age. I can remember as far back as five, but by seven I knew the name of Jesus and that there was a God. I was introduced to the name God and the name Jesus but had yet to meet either of them. I heard many stories about God and did the things I was told to do concerning the church.

As a child, I attended a well known North Philadelphia Catholic Elementary School. I remember when my sister and I would go to Mass. Before we could enter the sanctuary, we had to stop at a large marble bowl of water in the foyer area of the church and dip our finger in the water making the sign of the cross on our foreheads. After entering the sanctuary, when we came to the row that we were going to sit in, we had to stoop down, make the sign of the cross over our chests with our fingers and then proceed into the row to sit down. Though I was Baptist and was being raised as a Baptist, my mother at that time felt a good Catholic school education was necessary. She allowed my sister and me to attend Mass from time to time. I believe it was required for us in order to attend the school.

I also attended my family church. As a child my parents made sure we attended church as a family on a regular basis. We spent a lot of time in church. On Sundays after service, we would come home, have dinner and go right back to church. Sometimes we wouldn't even go home. We would eat at the church and go right into the next service. We lived right around the corner. If my parents and grandmother stayed, everybody had to stay. Church, church, church it seemed like that was all we knew. It was the normal and right thing to do.

Today my mother still sings with the choir but at a different church. My grandmother also still attends service. At ninety-three years of age she still tries not to miss a Sunday. After all these years it's still church as usual.

As a child, I remember sitting with my mother in the choir stand. Sometimes I would march up the aisle with her. We would march up the aisle as the congregation clapped their hands smiling while yelling, "Ya'll better go head." My mother sang and still does sing beautifully, she also plays the piano. We were members of The Southern Tabernacle Baptist Church in North Philadelphia. Those old Baptist Hymns are still rooted in me and will never die. Those were the days when before we got a piano, we didn't have any musical instruments. The old mothers and deacons of the church would start off with a foot stomp and a hand clap. Someone might join in with a tambourine. Bring in a little humming and we had ourselves a Holy Ghost party! If you want to spark a real Holy Ghost fire in the church today, just reach back and get one of those old Baptist Hymns that will remind you of just how good God is and watch a shout and a dance break forth.

I don't want to go too far back but one of my favorites is "Just another day that the Lord has kept me." I can sing that all day, changing the words every time I sing it. When you can praise God all by yourself, you can do it with or without music and with or without anybody.

Sometimes I attended church with my grandmother. She made sure she went if nobody else did. I remember holding her hand and holding on to her coat tail because she walked so fast.

My grandmother knew how to walk through the back alley ways of North Philadelphia as short cuts to get to a church. She knew all of the short cuts. I was afraid of the barking dogs but she wasn't.

I confessed Jesus Christ as my Lord and Savior, and was baptized at the age of nine. There was no sprinkling of water over my head; I was fully immersed in a baptism pool filled with water. I felt light when I came up out of the water. I was soaking wet but I didn't feel the weight of the water and my clothes. I remember my mother dressing me, my brother and my sister in all white. Even our socks were white. I didn't fully understand but I knew Jesus made people happy. As I grew older I only knew what I heard them say about Jesus. I kind of felt like I knew Him but I still had yet to meet Him.

Webster's dictionary defines the word meet; as a point of contact, to come upon, come into the presence of, an encounter, and to become acquainted with. I knew of God but was not acquainted with Him. At the age of nine, I was soon to have an encounter with His Holy Spirit.

My father was always reading the Bible. He made me read it too. He was a deacon and a trustee in the church that we use to attend. He took me with him to many church gatherings. Tent revivals were plentiful during my childhood years. I remember my father taking me to a tent revival where people were brought in on stretchers and in wheelchairs. It was one of many tent revivals we attended with the late Reverend A. A. Allen. I remember him very well; he was assisted by Reverend Don Stewart.

This was back in the late 1960's and early 70's. Reverend Allen was a powerful man of God. He would lay hands on people and they would tremble and sometimes pass out.

Today I know it as being slain in the spirit. He would take people who were sitting in their wheel chairs by their hands and they would get up and walk, start dancing, shouting and leaping with joy. They were acting very happy. I lifted my hands too. Like I see children do today, though they may not understand. At the time, I didn't understand but I did what I saw the adults do. I remember asking God what is making these people so happy? With my hands raised in the air I told God I wanted to feel what they were feeling. I wanted to be happy too. Suddenly, I felt a tingling feeling coming over me and I froze. I was afraid so I stiffened up. Immediately the feeling left me.

I know today that, it was the Holy Spirit. He is such a gentleman. He would never force Himself on anyone. You have to invite Him in and want to freely receive Him. Just as quickly as He came upon me, He was gone because I was afraid, but I had unknowingly asked for Him. In my innocence as a child, this was my first encounter with the Holy Spirit, but I still had yet to meet God. I came in contact with God's Holy Spirit but still didn't know Him. I never told anyone about that experience until I began to walk with God. At nine years old I wouldn't know how to explain that feeling. I just thought something strange was happening to me.

As a child, I didn't know who or how to tell an experience like that. How would I put it into words?

My father loved the Lord. He was always reading the Bible. He often came into my room, waking me up in the middle of the night to make me read scriptures. I shared my room with my older sister, but he didn't wake her up. I wanted to sleep and I hated when he would wake me up and make me read. He didn't care about what time it was. He would say "Mickie, get up and read this." He affectionately called me "Mickie" because my mom gave me ponytails that sat up high like Mickey Mouse ears. I didn't like that name but I still answered to it.

My father made me memorize the names of all sixty-six books of the Bible and I had to learn how to spell them correctly. I always had trouble spelling "Ecclesiastes." I could barely pronounce it and he wanted me to spell it. When I was outside playing, he would make me stop playing to go with him to a church or to a tent revival. Sometimes I would get angry, other times I was excited about going. I didn't always like it then but I'm glad about it today. It was my father who paved the road and laid the foundation for my meeting with God. My sister and I would sing the gospel songs from the albums he had purchased. We knew every song he would play. I'll never forget our little green record player we got for Christmas. You couldn't tell us anything, it had detachable speakers. We felt like big girls with the best stereo in the world.

I loved watching all the movies about Jesus Christ. There's an old version of the black and white movie named, "Jesus of Nazareth." I cried every time I watched this movie. I remember watching it with my little brother, he cried too.

Preparation can sometimes seem like a lifetime. I know now that I was definitely being prepared for something concerning the Lord. While growing up I always knew it was something different about me. I often talked to God when I didn't understand things. I would always ask Him a lot of questions. I just believed that He heard me, though He never answered me back. Maybe He did answer me back in different ways but as a child I was unaware of it. I asked a lot of questions because I was so in awe of His creation. I love nature, the ocean, flowers and I was so curious about all the different creatures on earth. The stars, the planets and how the universe was set were and still are so amazing to me. I knew I was different because I saw things differently. At the same time I thought something was wrong with me.

I mostly stayed to myself, being an introvert. I was a very shy child, always smiling. At times, I felt like I just didn't fit in. I didn't like crowds that much and I wasn't the life of the party. In fact, when I went to a party, I felt like I didn't belong. I was what people called a wall flower, someone who went to parties but did not dance. I didn't know how to dance but, I loved the music. If I was having fun, when the music stopped, I felt out of place like everyone was watching me. I wasn't a dancer, I knew a lot of people, but I didn't have many friends. I was fine with that because I didn't need more than two friends at a time. I always had just one or two good friends. That was all I needed because I enjoyed being by myself. Even they were the complete opposite of me. I would always do things differently, taking a different approach to things. I was always polite, mindful, and considerate. Into my adult years, I remained the same.

I was quiet and a loner but not lonely. Although introverted, I loved being outside anytime day or night. I just had to be out of the house, doing something or going somewhere. My mother always took my siblings and me places. We traveled a lot and had lots of fun. Whatever we did and wherever we went, the church was always a part of our lives.

I graduated from high school in 1977 at the age of seventeen. What I call my personal meeting with God came at the age of twenty-one. I never thought the meeting would take place the way it did or in the place that it did. After graduating, I moved out of my parent's house and I moved in with my aunt. My father was very strict and I needed room to breathe.

After moving in with my aunt, I wasn't going to church much. I basically went when I felt like it. I became like so many who grew up going to church on a regular basis but came out of the church once they left home. I only attended church on special occasions and holidays. I fell into the "Some of the time saints" category. Some of the time I went and some of the time I didn't. I went on Sunday's like Easter and Mother's Day just to name a few, but I was always in church on my knees praying when the New Year came in. In my mind it was still the right thing to do. I was kind of scared not to be in church on New Year's Eve. I felt like I at least owed God that much. I was thanking Him for the old year and praying that He would allow me to see another year. I didn't want to just make it over; I wanted to live to see the year through, with my health, my strength and my sanity. I was out of fellowship with God but He was always on my mind.

After moving in with my aunt, I started living like I wanted to live, and doing what the world did. The world lives any way they want to live and they do whatever they want to do. The world dances to the beat of a different drum and not to God's beat. All the while I felt like some of the things I was doing was not pleasing to the God the church told me about. In fact I knew some of the things I was doing was not pleasing to God; but I rested assured in knowing that if I asked for forgiveness, God would forgive me and that He would forgive me every time. That's what the church told me. That's what I did but I didn't think I had to change some of the ways I was living my life. On my way to commit the sin, whatever it was, I would ask for forgiveness in advance. I just hoped and prayed that the sky wouldn't part, and I didn't die while participating in the sin. I thought that as long as I was a nice person, didn't steal, treated people right and respected my parents, I was alright. God wouldn't send me to hell. I was so deceived. I was living reckless and close to the edge. I remembered some of what the Bible said but I didn't have a relationship or a real encounter with God, at least not yet.

I worked three years after graduating from High School before going to College. I would have gone sooner but I wanted to work and save some money. I started taking classes the winter semester of 1981. I worked full time during the day and went to school in the evening. At first it was hard adjusting after being out of the classroom for three years. I've heard people say go right to college right out of high school while your mind is fresh, but it wasn't too late. I was still young and I liked the thought of going to college.

I didn't participate in any groups or sororities at college. Like always, I stayed to myself, but I was tempted to join a group called "The Black Christian Coalition." This was the only group that got my attention. It was a Christian group that showed movies and hosted different affairs on the campus. One particular day they were handing out flyers to attend the viewing of a movie called "A Thief in the Night". The time of the movie showing just happened to be the same time as one of my classes. The message on the flyer pulled on my spirit so bad that I was contemplating cutting class. I was torn between the two. Going to class was the right thing to do but not going was about to change my life. I chose to see the movie.

I had no idea what was in store for me. I was about to experience true salvation and what it really means to be saved. I took a seat in the back of the classroom. It was a nice little crowd. Before the movie started, a pastor introduced himself, said a few words and a prayer. I said, "Amen" and the movie started. Back then they used the reel to reel 8mm movie films and projector. I don't think VCR's and VHS tapes were born yet. If they were I didn't know about them. The movie is based on the rapture and the second coming of Jesus.

The movie is based on the rapture and the second coming of Jesus Christ. It showed how if you did not receive Jesus Christ before the rapture you would be left behind on earth. Jesus would come for His people taking them to heaven to reign with Him forever. The movie showed that according to scripture, Jesus would come back like a thief in the night.

"But know this, that if the master of the house had known what hour the thief would come, he would have watched and not allowed his house to be broken into. Therefore you also be ready, for the Son of Man is coming at an hour you do not expect", Matthew 24:43, 44.

A thief comes quickly and disappears quickly and quietly. You know not when he'll come unless you're awake when it happens. The term, don't get caught sleeping, can be used from a spiritual perspective. Be awake and alert, expect the coming of Jesus. Not knowing when, should put some kind of fear in believers to keep us living right. The movie showed that after Jesus comes back for His people, those who were left behind would have to get what is called *"The mark of the beast"; "The mark is six, six, six", Revelation 13:15-18, 14:9-11.*

In order to get medicine, food and other necessary items you had to be branded with this mark. In the movie if you received the mark, you were confessing the Anti-Christ (devil) as Lord. If you refuse the mark, you would get your head cut off. After the rapture, renouncing the anti-Christ and claiming Jesus as Lord gave you another chance to make it into heaven, but it was going to cost you your head.

"...Then I saw the souls of those who had been beheaded for their witness to Jesus and for the word of God, who had not worshipped the beast or his image and had not received his mark on their foreheads or on their hands. And they lived and reigned with Christ for a thousand years," Revelation 20:4.

In the movie, the people who were left behind were not just nonbelievers, but they were hypocrites like I was at that time. I confessed Jesus but didn't live for Him. He was my Savior but not my Lord. I believed some of the things that the preacher said, but I really didn't open my Bible to find out for myself.

Having my head cut off was the part of the movie that frightened me the most. I wasn't about to lose my head to make it into heaven after Jesus Christ had already paid the price for me. He had already endured all the pain and suffering for me. Fear had never gripped me like that before. As I watched in horror, it was as if I felt the pendulum cutting off my head, as it cut off those people's heads in the movie. At that point, I was ready to do whatever that pastor told me to do. I was filled with anxiety, waiting for the next instruction. After the movie was over, some people immediately left the room. I guess fear drove them right out of the classroom. I was glued to my seat because I was too scared to move. Fear made me stay in that classroom. The pastor talked about how loving and forgiving God is. He explained that God doesn't send people to hell. We send ourselves to hell when we turn our backs on God and choose to live a life disconnected from our Father and Creator.

God gave us free will to choose life in Him and not death. The pastor went on to explain that hell was created for satan and his fallen angels and not for man, but you can't go to heaven if you don't want God. You can't go to heaven if you don't believe and receive His Son, Jesus Christ. There's just no getting around it.

There are no short cuts, no compromising, and no other remedy but confessing, believing and receiving Jesus Christ as Lord and Savior. Not the one or the other, but both Lord and Savior.

Here's a perfect example of what I'm talking about; you are waiting at the train station for the train to come. You see the train tracks and you believe and know without a doubt that the train travels on the tracks.

When the train arrives you have to have a ticket to get on. You know without a doubt that you have to have a ticket to get on the train but you say to yourself, "I know I need a ticket to ride this train but the conductor will let me go. I'll just get on and hopefully by the time the conductor gets to me, I would have already arrived at my destination."

That's how we treat God. We know there is a way to get to heaven, but we don't want to purchase the ticket. We want a free ride. The ride is free but Jesus is the ticket. He's already paid the price. God is the conductor and you definitely can't ride His train without that ticket. That's your only way in through the pearly gates of heaven. We want to live our lives the way we see fit and hope that we're the one God will let slip by, NOT.

What that pastor was saying sounded very rational to me. You can't come in my house if you don't respect who I am and abide by my rules. The pastor then asked if there was anyone who wanted to repent, turn away from their wicked ways and receive Jesus Christ as their Lord and Savior.

After a few minutes of explaining salvation he said, "Come to the front of the room if you want to receive Jesus." Something in me had never heard it the way this pastor was saying it. I know I had heard it many times before but not like this. I may have heard it but I had never received it the way I was receiving it at that time. Was I motivated by the movie? Absolutely, I certainly was and all that I remembered from a child up until that day came flooding back to me. They say that the apple doesn't fall far from the tree. However far I landed when I fell, my spot was about to be marked. I couldn't get to my feet fast enough to get to the front of that classroom. I raised my hands as that pastor began to pray for me and I began to feel the Holy Spirit consume my body inside out and outside in and then I began to weep. I cried like a newborn baby who just got smacked on the behind. Whatever burden and worry I was carrying at that time quickly vanished. There was such a cleansing and change taking place inside of me that when I walked out of that classroom, it felt like my feet were not touching the ground.

On my way home I felt like I loved everyone that passed by me. God's love was poured into me and was now flowing out of me. Hallelujah! I guess that's what it felt like when Peter was walking on the water. I had been cleansed of the flesh and was now walking in the spirit. My God, it's still so fresh in my mind. It was an experience I will never forget. It was an experience that will forever override any doubt whatsoever that Jesus is real, God is the Almighty Father and the Holy Spirit is indeed the Comforter abiding in us and with us on earth.

There are different things that take place in our lives that causes us to have an encounter with God. Saul, who became Paul in the New Testament, had such an encounter with God but under very different circumstances. Saul was a bounty hunter for Christians.

The Bible says *"As for Saul, he made havoc of the church, entering every house, and dragging off men and women, committing them to prison,"* Acts 8:3.

He entered into every house. He wasn't going to allow anyone to get away. Saul had the nerve to inquire of the high priest, letters to Damascus that gave him access to the synagogues to hunt and bind anyone who professed to know Jesus Christ. Saul slept, ate, walked, talked and breathed persecuting Christians. What he didn't know was that he was persecuting Christ who abided in the Christian. He did his job so well that the Lord Jesus had to pay him a very up close and personal visit. It was actually in his face.

It was on that road to Damascus that Saul had his meeting with Jesus. When the blinding light shined on Saul, though he didn't know Jesus he asked, *"Who are you, Lord?" Acts 9:5* He was frightened enough to address Jesus as Lord with fear and trembling. Saul was about to reap what he had sowed. God blinded his eyes and changed his name to Paul. He instructed Paul to go into a street called *Straight, Acts 9:11*.

THE MEETING | 13

The road to heaven is straight and narrow. I love this story. The reason God had to blind Saul's eyes was so that when he opened his eyes as Paul, he would see things differently.

When salvation comes, we can see through our spiritual eyes. We are blind to the things of God until we receive salvation. The song says, "I once was lost but now I'm found, was blind but now I see." Paul was lost, but God found him in a place that if the Lord had not intervened, Paul would have perished. He reminds me of a terrorist. He was faithful to what he believed was right even though it was wrong. In spite of what we do, God is super rich in mercy. His grace is immeasurable. When Paul received his sight, not only did he see differently, but his mind was renewed. His speech was changed; he had a new walk, a new talk and a brand new outlook on things. Now, he slept, ate, walked, talked and breathed the Gospel of Jesus Christ. When I get to heaven I'm sure Paul will tell me it was the best meeting he's ever had.

As children we meet God in church, vacation Bible schools, prayer camps, in the sandbox at the playground, while reading Christian books and in many other ways. I've seen babies lift their hands in the midst of a worship service, smiling looking up at the ceiling reaching out with their little hands. I know the angels have to be present. Children have such a vivid imagination; they are so innocent that they simply believe what adults tell them. They ask questions like, who is God. Where does He live? Why can't we see Him? How can He be everywhere at the same time? How come we can't hear Him? Adults tend to ask these same questions. Children have more sense than we give them credit for.

My girlfriend was sharing with me an experience she had with her three year old cousin. It was the Fourth of July and he was watching the fireworks.

He ran in the house to her and said, "There was fire in the sky." She asked him, "Where did it go?" He pointed his finger up and said, "It went up to God." Then he repeated what he had said. Though it was the cutest thing I had ever heard, I realized that someone had told this little boy something about God being in heaven and that heaven is up in the sky. It starts as a child. The seed you plant in your child's life is the harvest you will reap as they grow older.

Though *"Foolishness is bound up in the heart of a child, Proverbs 22:15,* like the small rudder that turns a big ship; with a small wheel, called the Bible, we can steer our children to meet and have an unforgettable encounter with a big God.

"Train up a child in the way he should go and when he is old he will not depart from it, Proverbs 22:6.

Thank you, Daddy!

The Day I Met God

I heard from a friend today
That God was a lot of fun
So I made a date with Him
To see if He would come
I picked the place to meet God
It was a blind date
I waited for Him to show up
Hoping He wouldn't be late
As I waited patiently
Under a beautiful tree
I thought I heard someone
Come and sit down beside me
I stretched out a blanket
Where the grass was fair
And then I felt a breeze
Blowing gently through my hair
It caught me by surprise
There was no blowing of the wind
As I looked around
Someone touched me on my chin

Up walked a gentleman
He stood tall like a tower
Stopping briefly in front of me
He passed me a rose flower
I wasn't far from the water
Just a few yards from the beach
When an ice cream truck drove slowly
Playing music down the street
Get your free ice cream here
Yelled a man who smiled at me
There was no one else around

As far as I could see
I was still waiting for God
To come and say hi
When suddenly a balloon
Fell from the sky
I was a little tired of waiting
As I sipped from a cup
I thought where are you God
Have you stood me up

And then a voice replied
I gave you a flower and
That was Me in the truck
It was My ice cream I shared
I was the breeze in your hair
And I touched your chin too
The balloon you now have
I sent it especially for you
I was always here
I can never be late
Anytime you want to be with Me
We can make it a date
I'm so glad you wanted to meet Me
I can be fun for you
But to get to know Me
Worship Me in spirit and in truth
I like having private time
With all my children on earth
I've set their end from the beginning
Even before their birth

I can't wait until the next time
When we come together again
Just be careful how you live and

Watch out for that thing called sin
The next time we'll take a walk
As you talk I'll always listen
Please don't wait too long
Because it's you that I'll be missing

2
Intimacy with God

Can intimacy with God be compared to intimacy with a man or a woman? In some ways, from a spiritual perspective it can be. Are you chasing God, or are you just satisfied with a usual fifteen minute Sunday sermon. Then when you get home, you can't tell anyone what the message was about?

Are you in love with God? Is he always on your mind? Do you find yourself talking to God when you are alone? Do you sometimes feel like you can't wait to get in His presence? Does your spirit feel ignited at the mention of the name Jesus? Do you feel like you just want to run because of His goodness? Do you have a burning desire to serve the Lord? If your answer is yes to any of these questions, then you must be in love with God.

David was in love with God; *"As the deer pants for the water brooks, so pants my soul for You, O God, My soul thirst for God, for the living God. Psalm 42:1-2".*

Do you thirst for God with a thirst that's only quenched by His presence? Intimacy with God is special; it's an overwhelming feeling of love. To worship God is a form of intimacy. Sitting quietly in His presence is a form of intimacy. Does your heart and soul long to be in God's presence when no one else is around, or do you only desire Him on a Sunday, or maybe on Wednesday night at Bible study? Do you open your Bible in church on Sundays only, while it collects dust at home Monday through Saturday? Or, do you experience intimacy with God through the constant reading of His Word? To fall in love with God is to fall in love with love.

When we fall in love or desire to be with that special man or woman, we run after them. We pursue them with whatever it takes. We send flowers, perfume or candy and take them to some of the most expensive restaurants in the city. We'll sometimes do whatever they want us to just to get in good with them or to impress them. Sometimes we spare no expense to win their love. It should be the same way with God. He spared no expense when it came to His Son. What price would you pay to save the world? Can one even add up the cost or imagine it with the human mind.

You will seek to pursue God in ways you have never known when you desire Him and are in love with him.

You will set a time to be only with Him, to read His Word or sing to His music. Yes, God does have His own music. It's a sound only you can hear.

The song He sings to me may be different from the songs He sings to you. There is a melody and harmony just for you. The Bible says that the Lord will rejoice over us with singing.

"He will rejoice over you with singing." Zephaniah 3:17.

When you're in love with God, you will chase Him with a pursuit that is untiring. I know all too well from experience that if you should get tired, the Lord will start the pursuit up again, by chasing you. A word or a song can drop in your spirit and set your soul on fire for God.

Obedience is an act of love. It is an act of worship. Obedience says Lord I'd rather make you happy than make you sad. When you meet that special someone and began to date them, after a while you began to feel comfortable enough with them to hold their hand. The two of you can't get enough of talking on the phone all hours of the day and night. You cannot get enough of being in each other's company. As the relationship grows, eventually, the two of you will exchange a kiss. Now, that man or woman has a piece of your heart. Who kisses just for the sake of kissing? Surely one or both must feel something for each other if there's a desire to kiss. The intimacy didn't just start with a kiss. Intimacy started when you first held that person's hand. A touch is a form of intimacy.

God desires the same thing. He desires to walk with us and talk with us. He wants us to read His word daily, even if you only have time to read a scripture, at least make the effort. The Word is so powerful a scripture can carry you all day and sometimes at the end of the day you will find that it was just the one you needed. When we read the Bible daily, we are being fed spiritually.

"Give us this day, our daily bread." Matthew 6:11. "It is written, Man shall not live by bread alone, but by every word that proceeds out from the mouth of God." Matthew 4:4.

When we read the Bible daily we commune with the Lord. Imagine kissing the face of God. When we commune with Him that's what we are doing. Would you send your child off to school every day or tuck them into bed every night without a kiss? There should be a feeling of joy when that love is demonstrated by a touch, a kiss or an, I love you.

When I read the Bible daily, the words began to come alive on the pages. God sometimes communicates with me by revelation through

His word. I get so excited sometimes I literally kiss the pages. I see it as a form of kissing God's face. Imagine being able to wrap your arms around God's neck. Can you see yourself hugging him? Imagine coming face to face with God spiritually as you worship; I guarantee you something will happen.

The mind is a powerful thing. I'm sure you've heard the term your imagination can run away with you. When it comes to God, let it. It's like free falling from an aircraft. Imagine being in the throne room of God, sitting at His feet. Being in God's presence can be so powerful that you cannot lift your head or open your eyes because of His glory. If you could, you just want to stay there in His presence. You will forget about work and anything else. You will not want to leave God's presence.

When a married couple first experience true marital bliss, they probably want to lie in each other's arms just a little while longer. If newlyweds have not had sexual relations with each other until their honeymoon night, my guess is that their orgasm as a married couple probably generated a tear or two. Deep feelings of intimacy will make you very emotional.

Intimacy with God will make you cry; long deep worship will open up your heart and allow God's love to flood in and through you. He will touch places in your heart you never knew existed. He will touch the core, the very soul of your being in a way only He can. A depth within you that only God knows exists. With each touch God will create in you a clean heart. He will renew your mind and your spirit and change everything about you.

I asked a friend, what was her most memorable experience of intimacy with God? She explained that while having lunch at work one day, she was enjoying a tuna fish sandwich and thinking about the Lord. Suddenly, she realized that she had fallen in love with Jesus. It hit her out of nowhere and she began to say aloud to herself "I have fallen in love with Jesus." She had been saved now for several years, a faithful church and Bible study attendee. She said she loved Jesus but didn't realize how much until she actually fell in love with Him. Her diligent worship, reading the Bible, prayer and fasting took her to another realm in God. She explained, "It was during that time that she became a friend of Jesus."

Jesus said to the disciples, *"No longer do I call you servants but I have called you friends," John 15:15.*

The Lord had made some things known to her because of her commitment and faithfulness to Him.

"You are my friends if you do whatever I command you", John 15:14".

My friend is so in love with Jesus that she has a ready "Yes Lord," to whatever His command is on her lips. She told me how she conversed with God daily and how they had lunch together and took walks together. When you're in love with someone, you want to talk to them daily. You want to feel their presence every day. You make time for them even if it means canceling out something on your schedule because they are more important to you. As she deepened her relationship with Jesus, the Holy Spirit had an answer for whatever she would ask. The Holy Spirit is a voice you never want to cease to hear. He's easily grieved so be careful how you handle Him. Be careful how you address Him and be careful and mindful where you take Him.

When we are in love, we whisper what we call "sweet nothings" in each other's ear. Come on, you know how we do. When we engage in conversation about the person we love, women say things like "Girl, he's all that and a bag of chips." Men say things like "Man, she's the sugar in my coffee." It's funny how we use food and other things to express our love for someone.

As for me, God is the coffee, cream and sugar in my cup. He's the cup that holds all three. In other words God is the glue that keeps my heart together, He is my all in all. God is not just first in my life, He is my life.

The Bible also uses food to express God's love for his children. We're referred to as the apple of his eye;

Psalm 17:8 "Keep me as the apple of your eye; hide me under the shadow of your wings.

Deuteronomy 32:10 "He found him in a desert land and in the wasteland, a howling wilderness; He encircled him, He instructed him, He kept him as the apple of His eye."

We love God because He first loved us, *1 John 4:19*. God is very concerned about how we treat each other. If God is love and He lives inside of us, why can't we love one another as God has commanded us to? The book of *1 John* expresses *"love in action"* and the *"source of love".*

Love in Action, I John 3:11-17

11 *For this is the message that you heard from the beginning, that we should love one another,*

12 *Not as Cain who was of the wicked one and murdered his brother. And why did he murder him? Because his works were evil and his brother's righteous.*

13 *Do not marvel, my brethren, if the world hates you.*

14 *We know that we have passed from death to life, because we love the brethren. He who does not love his brother abides in death.*

15 Whoever hates his brother is a murderer, and you know that no murderer has eternal life abiding in him.

16 By this we know love, because He laid down His life for us. And we also ought to lay down our lives for the brethren.

17 But whoever has this world's goods, and sees his brother in need, and shuts up his heart from him, how does the love of God abide in him?

The Source of Love, I John 4:7-21

7 Beloved, let us love one another, for love is of God; and everyone who loves is born of God and knows God.

8 He who does not love does not know God, for God is love.

9 In this the love of God was manifested toward us, that God has sent His only begotten Son into the world, that we might live through Him.

10 In this love, not that we loved God, but that He loved us and sent His Son to be the propitiation for our sins.

11 Beloved, if God so loved us, we also ought to love one another.

12 No one has seen God at any time. If we love one another, God abides in us, and His love has been perfected in us.

13 By this we know that we abide in Him, and He in us, because He has given us of His Spirit.

14 And we have seen and testify that the Father has sent the Son as Savior of the world.

15 *Whoever confesses that Jesus is the Son of God, God abides in him, and he in God.*

16 *And we have known and believed the love that God has for us. God is love, and he who abides in love abides in God, and God in him.*

17 *Love has been perfected among us in this: that we may have boldness in the Day of Judgment; because as He is, so are we in this world.*

It is only in Jesus Christ that we learn how to love, how to be in love and the true meaning of love.

18 *There is no fear in love; but perfect love casts out fear, because fear involves torment. But he who fears has not been made perfect in love.*

19 *We love Him because He first loved us.*

20 *If someone says, "I love God," and hates his brother, he is a liar; for he who does not love his brother whom he has seen, How can He love God whom he has not seen?*

21 *And this commandment we have from Him: that he who loves God must love his brother also.*

"For God so loved the world that He gave His only begotten Son, that whoever believes in Him should not perish but have everlasting life," John 3:16.

God did not just give His Son Jesus for us as a ransom; He gave Himself in the form of Jesus totally and unconditionally. To know God is to love God for He is indeed love magnified.

3
The Awe of God

The awe of God will leave you with a blank stare, trying to figure out what just happened and how. If you don't know God, I dare you to try Him. The awe of God will leave you speechless. God is and can be; unexplainable, amazing, mind boggling, indescribable and simply breathtaking. He's beyond what our finite minds consider magnificent, majestic and glorious as we know it.

I don't believe the human mind can contain the magnitude of His infinite wisdom and power. He's beyond miraculous as we know it. I'm a member of one of the most, powerful dynamic, raw, uncut, Bible teaching churches in the entire world. God visits us on a regular basis. The Lord uses my pastor, Bishop Jimmie A. Ellis III in a powerful way. He is a man of God with a transparent life. He's for God or nothing at all.

He is a very wise and knowledgeable teacher, skilled in the Word of God. Like an archer with a bow and arrow, he always hits his mark. He'll cut you off at the knees with the Word of God and then restore you with the love of God. He's like a surgeon. A surgeon has to cut you open to get to the root of the problem, inject you with medicine and then sew you back up. You'll get better with each Sunday morning visit from a follow-up service with Dr. Ellis III. After a surgeon has performed surgery on you, he gives you instructions to follow. He wants your surgery and your healing process to be a success. You have to follow instructions and take your medicine. You can't just take one pill and think that you're going to be alright, you will not be alright. You have to keep taking the medicine to get it into your system.

It's the same way with my pastor. After he gives us the message, we have to follow the instructions. We have to apply it to our lives so that it can bring about a change in our lives. You can't just come to one follow-up service and think that it's all you need. You have to keep hearing the Word of God until you get it in your system.

"So then faith comes by hearing and hearing by the Word of God". Romans 10:17.

I want to thank my Bishop at the end of every sermon. It's something in every message for me. When the atmosphere is set for God to have His way, anything can happen. I believe that if God didn't pull back His Spirit, we would probably keep praising Him until all of us pass out. We would be like lifeless bodies lying all around the sanctuary.

That's ok, but what are we going to do after we get up off of the floor? If we take what the man of God is teaching us and apply it to our lives, I guarantee we will see change. I'm a witness.

What we call a miracle is just a thought in the mind of God. All God has to do is think it and it's already done. If you've just stepped out of an ocean and God says it is a mountain and you know without a doubt it's an ocean because you just stepped out of, it will be a mountain. He can put an ocean in the desert and cause the sun to shine well into the night. I've seen the sun and the moon both out in the sky at the same time. How awesome is that? God spoke the world into existence and He holds all of creation by the power of His mouth. Life is in the power of the tongue. Hallelujah!

Imagine what it was like for Elisha to see the whirlwind, a chariot of fire with blazing horses and Elijah being translated into heaven.

11 Then it happened, as they continued on and talked, that suddenly a chariot of fire appeared with horses of fire, and separated the two of them; and Elijah went up by a whirlwind into heaven.

12 And Elisha saw it, and he cried out, "My father, my father, the chariot of Israel and its horsemen!" So he saw him no more. And he took hold of his own clothes and tore them into two pieces," 2 Kings 2:11-12.

Who would believe such a thing? Only a believer and someone who knows the power of their God would believe such a story.

What if one day you were walking along chatting with someone and suddenly, you found yourself walking through the gates of heaven, in an instant? You had no signs of illness, no pain and no warning, just an instant change. I think I'll ask Enoch what it was like when I get to heaven.

"And Enoch walked with God; and he was not, for God took him," Genesis 5:24.

Our minds cannot really conceive the awesomeness of God. He's sovereign, wonderful, delightful, beautiful and astonishing. There are not enough words in the English vocabulary or any vocabulary to describe how awesome God is. I believe that's why we cry and dance so hard and lift our hands toward heaven to try and embrace His awesomeness. It's how we express our love to Him. The awe of God is that no matter what you do or have done in your life time, with a repentant heart and a voice that asks for forgiveness, God will forgive your sins.

1 John 1:9, *"If we confess our sins, He is faithful and just to forgive us our sins and to cleanse us from all unrighteousness."*

Without the blood of Jesus Christ and the space to repent, hell would be our portion. God is so forgiving and long suffering. When it comes to patience, He knows all about it. Who can put up with the mess we continually display on the earth and throw in the face of God time and time again? God doesn't delight in suffering. He doesn't suffer forever, after a while like a parent He gives you fair warning and then comes the judgment.

It didn't feel good when our parents whipped us. God just whips us in a different way. He lets the consequences that follow our disobedience have its way. We tend to blame God just like we blamed everything on our parents for chastening us.

"For whom the Lord loves He chastens," Hebrews 12:6.

The awe of God can be expressed in many ways. It can be expressed by watching someone without arms, paint a full portrait with a paintbrush using his/her mouth. Having had arms and able to raise them to clap their hands to the glory of God, now being without arms using his/her mouth to raise a paintbrush and paint a picture. Painting portraits that glorify God.

The awe of God can be expressed in watching someone with no arms sing unto the Lord while playing a guitar with their feet. Only the miraculous power of God can touch the heart and mind of a man to perform such a gifted act. I was left in awe as I witnessed a man perform this on a Christian television show.

The awe of God is watching a baby born blind learn how to play a piano with understanding and no piano lessons at the age of two, with his ears and mind being a recorder of touch and sound. Today this person not only plays the piano but he sings and plays the trumpet as well. This is God on display. Only God can leave you wondering how.

"For the gifts and the calling of God are irrevocable," Romans 11:29, every gift still belongs to God and He's faithful to His covenant. We are fearfully and wonderfully made and His works are marvelous, *Psalms 139:14*.

The awe of God is looking out on the ocean and watching it meet the sky. Watching the beginning of the ocean waves roll in and roll out without the water ever overtaking the entire beach. It answers to the command that has already been put in place by the mouth of God. God commanded the waves to roll in to a certain point, stop and then recede.

Job 38: 11 "When I said, this far you may come, but no farther, and here your proud waves must stop!"

The awe of God is listening to a person sing with a voice that can shatter a glass. Only the power of God endowed upon us and in us can make one confess it is a gift from God. It is God that enables us to do the miraculous things that some of us can do and others cannot do. The list goes on and on but one cannot phantom the awesomeness of God until they experience God. God is so awesome that when he made a promise to Abraham, He had to swear by Himself.

"For when God made promise to Abraham, because he could swear by no greater, he swears by himself, Hebrews 6:13.

Who on God's green earth is greater than Him by whom to swear? No one not now or ever, what a mighty God we serve.

4
Drawn by God

God's plan for my life is a life of no lack, a life of abundance. It is life and abundance in all that concerns each and every one of us, not poverty or death.

Just looking at the world and how things are made should peak one's curiosity to want to know just how things became the way they are. How does a tiny little seed germinate and bloom into a beautiful flower? How does the seed push up through the weight of wet heavy dirt and become a color or many colors at the same time?

I believe all of God's creation has a command engraved in the very core of its life on this planet to do whatever He has commanded it to do. How do we explain the seven colors of the rainbow; the same exact colors every time, trapped in a place, side by side, not knowing where it starts or where it ends? Who can explain a double rainbow? I've seen a double rainbow twice in my lifetime.

I was on Amtrak on my way home from Florida the first time I saw it. I was so excited I began hitting my best friend on the leg without taking my eyes off of it. I said to her "look out the window, tell me you see this. Please tell me you see two rainbows." Sure enough she saw them.

I reached for my camera and started clicking away. I couldn't wait to get home and print those pictures out. After I printed them out you can clearly see both rainbows.

This was a type of experience that caused me to draw closer to God. When I was a hospital employee, I met God every day in the meditation room. I spent my lunch hour in this room faithfully every day. I remember coming out of the meditation room and waiting for the elevator to come. One day as the doors opened a man stepped off with a vase of beautiful flowers. He extended his arm and said "These are for you." I was elated. As he passed behind me, I turned to look at him from behind and just that quickly he was gone. That happened to me on two different occasions. I know they were Angels heaven sent. The Bible tells us to be kind to strangers because they may be an Angel.

That was one of God's way of saying, "I love you" after I had just finished loving on Him. It's the little things I appreciate so much. It's that little bit of time God appreciates from you. He appreciates all lengths of time but when you can appreciate the little things in God, the big things will not matter that much. You appreciate them no less but with me it's something about the little things God does that say He's thinking about me. When He does big things I'm just tickled pink. I love it when God makes me laugh.

Moses was drawn by God. He was determined to find out what or who was on top of that mountain. I'm not calling God a what, but Moses wanted to know what was making that mountain light up in the night. Moses was actually being drawn from the time he was a baby. His fate was sealed. He was drawn into the water by his mother so that his life would be spared. He was then drawn from the water so that his life was saved. God drew him to the mountain so that he could save the life of others. Even his name means; to draw out.

Exodus 2:10, "And the child grew, and she brought him to Pharaoh's daughter, and he became her son. So she called his name Moses, saying, "Because I drew him out of the water."

Though Moses was drawn to that mountain, he still had to move toward it. He still had to make an effort to go forward. He had to grab hold of that force that was drawing him. He didn't just hear a rumbling sound. He heard a voice speaking to his inner man and he had to pursue it.

The woman with the issue of blood was drawn by God. Though she is not named in the Bible, her story has impacted countless lives. When she heard that Jesus was coming, she made her way down through the village. Being weakened from the loss of blood for twelve long years, I assume she could not have had the strength in her legs to walk good in an upright position. She must have walked as best she could possibly, dragging herself along the ground, through the grass, through the dirt and over stones to get to Jesus.

She had to be low to the ground or actually on the ground, because one translation of the Bible tells us that she touched the border, (hem) of Jesus garment.

The robes of the days of old were worn long and some of them probably touched the ground. Jesus robe was probably just as long and also touching the ground. She had to be close to the ground because the disciples didn't even see the woman, neither did Jesus see her. If He did He wouldn't have asked the disciples "Who touch me." The Bible says "When she heard about Jesus she came behind him in the crowd." The disciples said to Jesus, you see this crowd pressing up against you and you asking us who touched you. How are we supposed to know, they're pressing up against us too? They sounded a bit sarcastic to me.

Mark 5:27-31, "When she heard about Jesus, she came up behind him in the crowd and touched his cloak

28 because she thought, "If I just touch his clothes, I will be healed."

29 Immediately her bleeding stopped and she felt in her body that she was freed from her suffering.

30 At once Jesus realized that power had gone out from him. He turned around in the crowd and asked, "Who touched my clothes?"

31 "You see the people crowding against you," his disciples answered, "and yet you can ask, 'Who touched me?'"

I know that this woman was in a standing position after she was healed because that's when Jesus spotted her. She was standing, afraid because she was no longer hidden and she didn't know what Jesus would say. It seems to me as though she was just going to get her healing, blend in with the crowd, and stroll away without so much as a thank you to Jesus. I know she was standing because the Bible tells us that she fell down,

"Then the woman, seeing that she could not go unnoticed, came trembling and fell at his feet. In the presence of all the people, she told why she had touched him and how she had been instantly healed." Luke 8:47.

This was after Jesus turned around and knew it was her who had touched Him. It was what this woman heard about Jesus that drew her, but it was her faith that pushed her. She could not see anything but that healing virtue drawing her, beckoning her, calling her by name. It was her day and her time.

All she had to do was believe and follow what she believed for, but she had to make a move. She couldn't just stay in her house saying, "I believe God for my healing", and do nothing. She had to do something. She had to start moving toward whatever it was going to take to get her healing. She had to move. When you are drawn by God, you have to move. The Bible says the Lepers were healed as they went. They couldn't just stand there they had to move before they could see the manifestation of their healing. The manifestation happened as they were walking and when they realized it, only one returned to Jesus to say thank you.

"So when He saw them, He said to them, "Go, show yourselves to the priests. And so it was that as they went they were cleansed", Luke 17:14.

In the book of Esther, like Moses, Esther too was drawn by God to save her people from outright murder, destruction and almost becoming extinct. If Esther had not been bold enough to go before the King, even risking her life, she and her people would have perished. Esther had to move in spite of what could have happened to her, having faith and knowing that God already knew what would happen.

I'm reminded of a scene from the movie Forrest Gump. He was being chased by his enemies. They were bullies. He could hardly run because of the braces on his legs. He couldn't bend his knees so Forrest began to take steps in little leaps. He lifted his steps higher and higher until he ran right out of those braces. He ran right out of his affliction but he had to make a move. He had to make his legs move. It was fear that caused Forrest to take off and run. Fear can sometimes be a good motivator. At some point and time something in life ought to motivate us to change. Change how we live and change how we do things. It doesn't have to be fear.

In *Luke 19:2-9,* Zacchaeus had to move. Because he was too short to see Jesus through the crowd, he had enough determination to climb a Sycamore tree so that Jesus could see him. The Bible tells us that he ran ahead of the crowd to where Jesus would pass by. Zacchaeus didn't just move, he ran. As a result salvation came to his house. Jesus told him

"*Zacchaeus, come down immediately.*" Jesus was telling him to hurry up it's your turn, don't miss it. Hallelujah!!!

I feel the anointing on that. Like Forrest, sometimes we have to run. If you move too slow you might miss your time and your turn.

In the book of John, the blind man had to move. Even though Jesus used His saliva to make clay from the dirt and lay it on his eyes, he still had to move. Jesus told him to GO!

Go where, "*Go and wash in the pool of Siloam.*" The Bible tells us that "*So he went and washed, and came back seeing*", John 9:6-7. How did he know where the pool of Siloam was, he was blind? It doesn't say that Jesus or anyone escorted him there and "*Then he came back.*" Jesus gave him specific instructions and he moved according to the instructions. What would have happened if the blind man had just sat there with the anointed clay on his eyes? He would still be blind. The manifestation of his healing came when he decided to move by faith. When God gives you instructions, you have to move. It is granted unto you according to your faith.

When God begins to draw you, you have to be sensitive enough to move at his beckoning. God can and will draw you right out of whatever's got you bound. I believe that every experience with God is an unforgettable experience. I believe that God is so powerful that however He chooses to draw you or however you meet Him, you will, without a doubt, know that you have just come in contact with the Spirit of the Lord. One thing I know for sure is that whether it's in your bedroom, your kitchen, at the Mall, or even in your car, God will meet you wherever you are.

He's already everywhere all the time, just waiting for you, but first you must believe. No man can come to Christ except he be drawn by God. You must believe.

"But there are some of you who do not believe", "Therefore I have said to you that no one can come to Me unless it has been granted to him by My Father", John 6:64, 65.

After Jesus said these words, the Bible says that many of His followers turn and went the other way. Jesus already knew who believed and who did not.

Jesus said *"Behold, I stand at the door and knock: If any man hears my voice and opens the door, I will come into him and dine with him, and he with me", Revelation 3:20.*

God is knocking at the door of His human creation's heart, just waiting patiently for all men to open their hearts and receive Him. God will give you unspeakable joy. There is nothing that a man or woman can say, show you or give to you that can make you more happy and ecstatic than you can ever imagine, but God. That is a joy that only God can give to you. It is a kind of love and joy that is unmeasurable, so unexplainable and so phenomenal that you won't be able to put it into words. If you want to know the love that God has for you, then maybe you should show God the love that you have for Him.

Deep calls unto deep, Psalms 42:7. I desire the deep things of God therefore I press to know more of God today, than I knew of Him on yesterday.

When you desire the deep things of God, it's like being on a quest to find a precious treasure. Its riches are untold. A treasure hunter never ceases searching for treasure. Year after year, after year, after year they continue to search.

After having found treasure after treasure, after treasure, after treasure, what are they still looking for? You may have heard the term, "the mother lode". Well, that's the one that set's them up for life. Regardless of how many people they have to split the findings with, it's enough for everybody to retire on. After that, they don't have to look no more. They will be set for life.

There are so many things about God that we don't know. The more I find out about God, the more I want to find out about Him. Our map is the Bible. There's a treasure on every page, and on every page, if you follow, it leads to "the mother lode." It's where you will be set for life. The Bible draws you to many different places in God; the ultimate treasure is heaven where the streets are paved with gold. Where treasures we can't imagine are untold. It's a type of, *"pure gold that's transparent like glass, Revelation 21:21".* That's the kind of treasure I long to behold. It's not the treasure that I'm after; it's the owner of the treasure. Let the owner of the treasure capture you and the treasure is yours.

The Bible says, "no man can come to Jesus except he be drawn to him by God", John 6:44. He that comes to God must first believe that he is and that he is a rewarder to them that diligently seek him, Hebrews 11:6. How does God reward you?

What does He reward you with? His rewards are unending. God rewards you with salvation and everlasting life, through His son Jesus, the greatest gift of all. With that gift comes a greater sense of love, peace and joy.

5
Dating God

I have no doubt that a man should always act like a gentleman towards a woman. Women should be treated like the queens we are. If men treat us right, we'll make them the happiest man in the world. If they treat us wrong, we can make them the saddest man in the world. I believe women have a lot of power naturally and spiritually. We just need wisdom on how to channel it in the right direction. Now I know there are some good men in the world who have treated their women like queens and some women have broken their hearts. The same can be said about women.

Personally I believe a real man will always treat a woman with the utmost respect. From what I have witnessed, when a man treats his mother right, he will do the same for the woman in his life. As for me, I prefer an intelligent man with a sense of humor. Though I'm very serious about my life and life in general, I like to laugh.

The sound of laughter can change the atmosphere. It helps if he is a little sensitive too. I like an extremely romantic man who can still be as masculine as he wants to be, but be able to shift into that mushy I'm deep in love with you mode. He has to be able to bring balance to our relationship. Yes, of course looks matter, you better believe it.

He doesn't have to be the most handsome person in the world, but he definitely has to have some handsome qualities. Oh, and don't forget the surprises, keep them coming. I like surprises and enjoy surprising as well, but basically I'm a homebody. I like to cook a fabulous dinner, cuddle up and watch a movie. Don't forget the most important thing; he has to know my God. Not just know of Him, but have a relationship with Him.

When we are dating, we seek the affection, attention and heart of another. Dating in the natural can be compared to what I will call dating God spiritually. However, I don't believe God can be dated. He is a jealous God. Either you are with Him or you are not. You don't spend an evening with Him and then drop Him off afterwards. He's not somebody you handle at curb side. He's the best and He deserves the best. The best what? The best of all you can give Him. He is always there. He will never leave you or forsake you and He expects the same commitment and devotion from us.

The Holy Spirit is a Gentleman. He understands our hurts, our rejections, and our disappointments. He's sensitive to our needs. He kisses our tears away and He will hold us in His arms all night if he has to. He is the Comforter and He releases that comfort in our time of need.

Therefore a date with God really can't be compared to a date in the natural. What or who can be compared to God? There is simply none like Him. Who can hold your hand like He can and change your life with a touch? Who can hold you like He can and a peace that surpasses our understanding comes over us? He can cause the wind to blow on your face in a way that you will know it was something about that breeze. He is the wind in your hair. He's a cool breeze on a hot steamy night. His sweet nothings are not like mans, they are always something special when He whispers in your ear and He's faithful to whatever He says. Who wouldn't want to love and serve a God like this?

What is it that is keeping us from giving God the attention He rightfully deserves? Who is that someone or something taking up quality time that belongs only to God? Is it our job? How much overtime do we put in for a few dollars more and still can't make ends meet. Is it that favorite television show, hanging out at the Mall or just doing nothing? Are we squeezing God into our schedule or should we be squeezing our schedule into the time we spend with God?

I love God so much that there are times when I just sit and talk to Him. I'd ask Him, Lord who broke your heart today? Was it me Lord? Who has made you cry today? Was it me Lord? I apologize and repent of the sins that I have knowingly and unknowingly committed against You Lord." Whether I sinned outright or just in my mind, I owe God an apology every day. I owe Him a thank you and praise every day. What would happen if God cried? What would happen if just one of His tears fell to the earth? It would probably have an atomic, nuclear bomb affect causing a supernatural Tsunami wiping out the entire world. Imagine that, the awesome power of a tear from God. Frightening isn't it?

There is no dating God, only an everlasting relationship with Him. Either you are with Him or you are not. It's that simple, but try not to break His heart.

6
The Marriage

After you have met God the zeal and the excitement you are feeling is overwhelming. You cannot get enough of going to church. You find yourself wanting to be there every time the church doors open. You want to say "Yes" to every auxiliary that asks you to join. The name of Jesus is always on the tip of your tongue, and now it seems like you just cannot hold a conversation without mentioning His name.

You find yourself spending an unlimited amount of time in God's presence, reading the Bible and anything else that you can get your hands on, that represents Jesus Christ. Television hardly exists anymore as a part of your daily activities. Fasting and prayer have now become a vital part of your life. Surprisingly, you probably never thought that you could go so long without food. You have fallen in love with Jesus and refuse to date anyone else but Him. You have now vowed that you are married to God, and that Jesus is your husband.

What does it mean to be married to God? As a single Christian, He is not just first in my life but He is my life. All else is second to God and the plan God has for my life.

1 Corinthians 7:32-34, "He/she that is unmarried cares for the things

that belong to the Lord, how he/she may please the Lord, being holy both in body and in spirit."

Marriage is a ministry, even in God. As God ministers to us, we in turn are to minister to Him. We can minister to the Lord in different ways. We can minister to the Lord by;

"Speak to one another with psalms, hymns and spiritual songs. Sing and make music in your heart to the Lord, always giving thanks to God the Father for everything, in the name of our Lord Jesus Christ.", Ephesians 5:19, 20.

Husbands are to minister to their wife's needs and wives are to minister to their husbands needs. Women are supposed to be a helpmeet to their husbands, meeting every need, submitting to their husband and their marriage. According to Proverbs chapter 31, a virtuous woman is a woman who knows how to minister to her husband and her family's needs. *Proverbs 31:11,"Her husband has full confidence in her and lacks nothing of value.*

12, "She brings him good, not harm, all the days of her life.

Verse 12 sounds like a woman who knows how to minister to her husband, mentally, emotionally as well as physically. She knows the right words to say while not withholding any good from him. She's not nagging or complaining about what he is or is not doing, nor what he should or shouldn't be doing.

Three things a man hates is a nagging, complaining, discontented woman. My father would make me laugh when he would say my mother keeps nagging him. It was the way he said it that was funny, it was no bitterness in his voice. He nagged her too. They were both funny.

Proverbs 21:19, "Better to live in a desert than with a quarrelsome and ill-tempered wife."

THE MARRIAGE | 47

Verses 13-17, I would suggest that this woman reads and prays to keep her faith strong. She is intelligent and must exercise daily. Verse 17 says she strengthens her arms. She is sure of herself and confident in her capabilities, buying, investing and turning a profit. She already has it going on because she has house servants and she readily provides for them. She's a good employer.

13 She selects wool and flax and works with eager hands.

14 She is like the merchant ships, bringing her food from afar.

15 She gets up while it is still dark; she provides food for her family and portions for her servant girls.

16 She considers a field and buys it; out of her earnings she plants a vineyard.

17 She sets about her work vigorously; her arms are strong for her tasks.

Verse 18 says that "She sees that her trading is profitable, and her lamp does not go out at night."

This wife is educated and has skill. She speaks eloquently and knows how to market her product. Verse 27, implies that this wife does not have time for petty gossip and she does not procrastinate.

She uses her time wisely, to structure, to build and to fortify all that concerns her, her family and her household.

"She watches over the affairs of her household and does not eat the bread of idleness.

Verse 28-31 tells us how her children call her blessed and her husband praises her also. There's nothing like a happy child that is grateful to their mother for all that she does for them. A happy child is an obedient child. They don't mind doing their daily chores. They know they have already been rewarded. They are happy with the example their mother sets for them. These children don't mind bragging about having the best mom. Her husband boasts of her and praises her. Who this woman is, how she conducts her business and run her household speaks for itself, her character is rewarding. Her husband goes to work a happy man every day. He probably whistles all the way home anxious to get home to his wife and children. A well kept man is a happy man. He doesn't mind going home every day.

I'm sure he is envied in his town. The men at the gate probably talked amongst each other about how blessed this man is. They probably wished they were in his shoes. The whole chapter of Proverbs 31 teaches a woman how to minister to her husband's and children's needs.

How much more would a man want to do right by his wife? Or shall I say I wouldn't understand why a man wouldn't want to do right by his wife. This virtuous woman was upright and her husband was highly favored by God and man.

"He who finds a wife, finds what is good, and receives favor from the Lord," Proverbs 18:22.

God loves us like that. He wants to provide our every need so that we can be a blessing to others. He wants us to brag and boast about how good He is and how we are nothing and can do nothing without Him.

As a single woman, I have yet to experience marriage. I sometimes compare my relationship with God to that of a married couple. I love the book of the Song of Solomon in the Bible because his words of love and affection are powerful. They are symbolic to me as a single woman in love with God. God has a passionate love for us. We in turn should have a passionate love for God. We should desire to serve Him with our whole heart and be obedient to His Word.

THE MARRIAGE | 49

Marriage between a man and a woman is bound by a covenant. They become one. As a single woman, I'm in covenant with God. As a Christian, I'm in covenant with God. God and I don't have a contract. Contracts can be made null and void. Contracts can be broken. A covenant is binding for life. My heart belongs to Him. I'm committed and submitted to Him because He loves me and He loves me unconditionally.

1 Corinthians 7:32, 33 "I would like to be free from concern, an unmarried man is concerned about the Lord's affairs, how he can please the Lord". But a married man is concerned about the things of this world, how he can please his wife.

Song of Solomon 4:10,"How delightful is your love my sister, my bride. How much more pleasing is your love than wine......" King Solomon is not talking to God. King Solomon was talking about the passion and lovemaking between him and his woman. I apply it to myself from a spiritual sense. God shows and allows me to experience His love in many different ways. The taste of the Lord is better than a sip of wine. I have tasted and seen that the Lord is better than good.

I remember going into my closet to pray. It's large enough for me to walk in, kneel down or sit comfortably inside to pray. I just wanted to talk to my Father, my Lord. I felt a tugging in my spirit that God also desired to talk to me. As soon as I closed the door, I could feel His presence. An overwhelming feeling of joy had come over me. I was feeling tingly all over. I got down on my knees smiled and began to talk casually to the Lord. From casual talking, I shifted into prayer mode. I began praying in English and then in my spiritual language speaking in tongues.

My prayer went back and forth from English to tongues. The Holy Spirit gave me the utterance and the interpretation of what I was praying. I began to stand to my feet and I started singing in the spirit. As I stood upright, I began to sway back and forth.

My singing became quieter and I felt a hand gently take my hand and an arm gently come around my shoulder. I was no longer singing but I could hear a sweet sounding music.

I kept my eyes closed as I laid my head on His chest. I felt the Lord's embrace and we began to dance with each other in my closet. We waltzed together and I will never ever, ever forget that precious unforgettable experience with my Lord. That was an, I love you so much, that I would come down and dance with you moment. It is forever mine and no one can take it away from me. It was up close and very personal. Yes, you can feel God if you'll just open up your heart and your spirit to Him. When you have a personal relationship with the Lord, He will let you experience Him in a very up close personal way. Of course after that experience, I fell deeper in love with the Lord. All you have to do is invite Him to come in and He will fellowship with you.

That passion and love that fills a marriage can be had with God. It's a heavenly sensation; it will drive you further into His presence. It's the kind of love and passion that you think it, you breathe it, you walk in it and you live it. In that place, you are completely out of yourself and into Him. You dwell in that place and you find safety, comfort, strength, love, joy, peace and answers to your problems. There is nothing but an atmosphere of positivity in every area you can think of in that special place. It's a place you long to stay; a place where you know nothing outside of that realm can touch you. It is a place where the Holy Spirit holds the keys to open all doors. Where is that place? You mark it and make it the place where you will seek God and where you expect Him to meet you. '

If you seek to meet with Him, I guarantee He will show up. He'll be waiting for you before you even get there. Find your place, mark it and try not to keep God waiting.

7
Broken Vows

The Bible clearly states that *"Marriage should be honored by all and the marriage bed kept pure, for God will judge the adulterer and all the sexually immoral", Hebrews 13:4.* Committing adultery against your husband or wife is just like committing adultery against God. Marriage is ordained by God. God takes marriage very seriously, His and others.

We commit adultery against God in different ways. Our lust for worldly things is a type of adultery. Notice, I did not say love for worldly things. God wants us to have things but don't let the things have you. He doesn't want us to worship things. Don't make things your idols. Idols can't bless you or heal you and they certainly can't give you everlasting life. You can call on the name of that idol but it can't hear you. It's not in what you call on but it's in who you call upon. It's not in what you know but it's in who you know. I only know one name that I can call on and get immediate results.

No, it's not mommy or daddy, it's the name Jesus. Mommy and daddy can help but Jesus can fix it. Mommy and daddy can put a band aid on it but Jesus can heal it.

God wants us to have a healthy, prosperous, successful life. He wants us

52 | DRAWN BY GOD

to enjoy being here on earth and all that He's provided for us. He enjoys us. We were created for His pleasure and we should enjoy the things on earth in which we find pleasure in. Let me be clear, our focus should be in those things that are pleasing in His sight. It's funny how we find the most pleasure in some of the things that are not pleasing to God. Sometimes that can be the enemy at work. The devil is so cunning. He can make the very thing you know is ugly, look good. The very things you know you don't want to do, you find yourself doing them anyway.

The Bible tells us to *"Do not handle, do not taste, do not touch, Colossians 2:21".*

What shouldn't we touch, taste or handle; those things that defile our minds and spirits. We can include the natural side of our being as well. We should not touch, taste or handle those things that hinder our spiritual growth. We should not touch, taste or handle anything that shames the God we represent. As Christians our lifestyle before the world should mean the world to us. Why would the world want to follow us if we're doing the same things they're doing. Where is the Christ like behavior and how do we win them over to Jesus?

God is a jealous God and it is written that "You shall have no other gods before Me, Exodus 20:3".

4   *You shall not make for yourself an idol in the form of anything in heaven above or on the earth beneath or in the waters below.*

5   *You shall not bow down to them or worship them, for I the Lord your God am a jealous God punishing the children for the sins of their fathers to the third and fourth generation of those who hate. Exodus 20:4-5".*

It was after God handed down the Ten Commandments to Moses on Mount Sinai that Moses said to the children of Israel;

"God is come to test you so that the fear of God will be with you to keep you from sinning. Exodus 20:20".

God will prove your love for Him through your obedience. Do you believe, trust and obey God or do you just want the blessings and not the Blessor? Either way God knows your heart, or He will bless whomever He chooses to. In the natural we can pretend to love someone because of what we know we can get but we really don't even like the person. That's false love. With God it is false love and false worship. Your whole motive is false. Forget the blessing; a curse is what you will bring on yourself.

God will never leave us or forsake us, although we cheat on Him, we lie to Him and we sin against Him over and over and over again.

We rebel against God and we are disobedient. We disappoint Him and break our vows to Him almost on a daily basis. I know we don't always bat a thousand because this Christian walk is not easy. We backslide and yet God is still faithful and forgiving to us. I'm so glad He understands. Thank God for brand new mercy daily.

Every day He gives us a chance to get it right. He gives us a chance to do better than we did yesterday. With open arms God is ready to scoop us up with His undying love, mercy, compassion and forgiveness. Even before we ask, He's already heard us. What a powerful impact this kind of love and forgiveness can have in a marriage. How much more excellent can a couple's life be if they could just stay true to each other as God stays true to us. I know there is no perfect marriage because we are not perfect beings. God doesn't expect perfection out of us but He does expect us to strive to be the very best we can be in Jesus Christ, loving one another.

"Husbands love your wives, just as Christ loved the church and gave Himself up for her, Ephesians 5:25".

The woman is taken out of the man and shaped in the physical image like man but with a different body structure and anatomy. Who would do harm to himself? There's a saying "Would you cut off your nose to spite your face?" Would your face respond "Why did you cut off my nose"? It sounds funny but it isn't. By the same token, every time a husband calls his wife a name, he's calling himself a name because she is him. Every time a wife withholds sexual intimacy from her husband she denies herself.

The devil loves it when married couples argue and deprive each other. That opens the door to the devil and gives him the opportunity to cause the husband or the wife eyes to wander. The spirit of lust is just waiting to present itself to one or the other. When a third person is invited into the marriage, it divides what God has joined together. The vow to be faithful has just been broken. Amidst all of the hurt, and the pain, the breaking of one vow can lead to the breaking of many.

Dishonesty and distrust work hand in hand. Anything with a "**dis**" in front of it will all meet up. These all follow closely behind. **Dis**respect; **dis**sin one another; becoming **dis**associated with responsibilities towards one another, being inconsiderate; **dis**regarding one another, and still being in a marriage relationship, acting like roommates instead of husband and wife; **dis**appearing; instead of coming home to one another and not so much as a phone call. We expect this much from our children; not using any **dis**cretion; ultimately the child suffers the **dis**advantage of a divided family; and the list goes on and on.

Sexual contact with another person is one of the most powerful intimate experiences we can have. It can be like an addict on drugs. I've heard some addicts say their love for the drug and its high is better than having sex. Sex will hold you hostage for a ransom that can't be paid. If I may be frank, we like it because it feels good but what feels good is not always good for us. Oh, I can tell the story but I won't, at least not this time. The things we'll do for sex and what we think is love.

Continual fornication for a single person in or out of the body of Christ will cause a soul tie. I'm a witness. A soul tie is like a threefold cord that is not easily broken. If you are single, don't allow the Christ in you to be raped. That's exactly how I felt when I fell into sexual sin. Thank God, where sin abound, grace abound that much more. In my experience I found that sexual sin will put a tear in your spirit, a gaping hole that runs deep with the stigma of everyone that person has slept with and all the people they have slept with. As a Christian, fornication will disrupt your life if you continue in it as a lifestyle. It's not just in the sexual act that you develop a soul tie. Soul ties are developed in different ways with different people.

When I fell into sexual sin, I felt dirty and stained. Even as I showered it was something that I couldn't wash off. I was angry with myself for allowing it to happen. Was I prayed up? Yes, or at least I thought I was. I found out you can come right out of prayer and fall into sin. You can come right out of a powerful church service and cuss like a sailor. This stinking flesh will never be saved. I wanted to peel mine off and throw it up on the altar. I should have never gone for the ride in that car. Forget the ride; I should have never answered the door. You can't play with the devil, before you know it you'll be asking yourself. "What have I done?" What I couldn't physically wash off in the shower got washed away with the blood of Jesus. I carried the guilt and the shame. I carried the shame of wanting to tell but didn't know who I could trust to tell. It seems like some church people in the church enjoy telling hurting people's business.

I was so messed up that the angels had to come down and minister healing to me. The Holy Spirit comforted me while the devil made me feel like I couldn't tell anyone. I had to tell it, it was eating me up. I felt so ashamed that I told it the next day. I had already qualified someone whom I could confide in. I needed prayer, not scolding. This was not a lifestyle; I got caught up with the same devil from my past for one night.

One night was all it took to shake my soul to the core. I had to quickly expose the devil before it had a chance to happen again. If you make a mistake, don't wait, waiting only makes it harder to tell. Sever the tie before it gets too strong. Sever it at the root. TELL IT!

Have you ever wondered why it might be so hard for you to stay away from someone you hate being around? You don't even like them, but you've done some things with that person in times past and you have a history with them. Or, you like being around a person but you know they are no good for you. You just can't seem to stay away from them. It's because you have developed a soul tie. Soul ties can be good or they can be bad. In the Bible, Jonathan and David had a good soul tie. They were spiritually connected, knitted together for a purpose. How many meaningless relationships have we been in? It was wasted time that we can't get back. How much of ourselves have we given to the wrong person, who kept on taking and taking and never giving anything back, leaving us emptier and emptier every time they departed from us?

When one wounded spouse leaves the other, there's a feeling of loneliness. When we leave God, we wound Him and He yearns to fellowship with us. We can leave each other but we can never escape the love of God. We have free will and God will never force Himself on us. If that was the case, then we would be like robots. We would be mechanical in our worship which would still be false. We need to give of ourselves more, more to God and more to each other. Forsake our selfish ways and consider the other person. Not just in marriage but in general as well.

How many good deeds go undone because of a selfish attitude? How many lives could have already been impacted if, when the opportunity presented itself, all we had to do was act on it? A person who has that "It's all about me mentality", will find themselves in a place always thinking that the world and everybody in it owes them something, and when the rude awakening is over, it can be devastating. When should it be about you? When you consider others? Life without Jesus is hard enough but by faith we know that; *"I can do everything through Him that gives me strength."Philippians 4:13.*

Be careful when you make a vow to God. When you vow to serve the Lord, be as a Nazarene; separated and consecrated unto Him. You cannot do what you want to do and you cannot go wherever you want to go. Even when it comes to witnessing, sometimes you have to be led by the Holy Spirit.

We break our promises and vows to one another all the time. We hope that the person never finds out about the lie, what we did or what we didn't do. When a spouse commits adultery, there is a combination of all kinds of feelings going off at the same time. I'm sure the deep hurt and betrayal runs deeper than I can imagine. In my early adulthood, I know how I felt when my boyfriend cheated on me. But that hurt and anger gave me the strength to say "Get to step-in; we have nothing to talk about." He was just a boyfriend. In my immature state of mind, I hollered next!

It's something different when it's the husband or the wife that's committing the adultery. What exactly do those wedding vows mean to them? What is each individual willing to give of themselves or give up for the other to maintain that which is most honorable in the sight of God? How hard is it to stay married until death do you part? Surely with God it has to be much easier than without God. The Bible tells us that a man who commits adultery lacks understanding. He destroys his own soul, he will be dishonored and his reproach will not be wiped away, *Proverbs 6:32-33.*

My parents were married for forty-nine and a half years. It was death that parted them. My father passed on first. It was plenty of storms they had to weather. They chose to weather them together. There was no cussing, fighting and drinking going on in my home, thank God. My mother didn't allow it. She didn't allow my father to keep any alcoholic beverage in the house. They were not drinkers and my father couldn't even keep a beer in the refrigerator.

My mother always felt like if it's in the children's sight, they will be tempted to try it. I strongly agree. What we did on our own was another story, but I believe sometimes parents aware and unaware contribute to our children's behavior and their addictions. A parent might put the first drink in their hand celebrating that eighteenth birthday party, some even younger than eighteen.

My parents didn't allow certain things to go on in our home. We couldn't bring something new in the house if we didn't have a job to buy it, and if we did we had to prove where it came from. My parents set the standard and we followed. We couldn't suck our teeth, roll our eyes, or pout and get away with it. The rod had its place in my home and it found its way to our backsides whenever it was needed. The sacred belt never wore out. Was it always peaches and cream, no but even if they didn't like each other for a day, the fear of God and those spoken vows must have run deeper and deeper with each passing year. I appreciate the fact that my parents never considered divorce. It was not an option. The love of our family was always first. Those core family values have kept us a close knit family. As for me and my house, we will serve the Lord.

My friend told me she asked her husband what was it about her that causes him not to look at another woman. They have been happily married for many years. Her husband told her that it had nothing to do with her or her beauty, he simply feared God. Wow! What a way to stay in check. The fear of the Lord will keep you in line, if you let it. God honors faithfulness and He honors your obedience.

God appreciates and honors your obedience more than your sacrifice. That's why the Bible tells us that your obedience is better than sacrifice. Consequences follow disobedience sometimes in the worst way.

"......Does the Lord delight in burnt offering and sacrifices as much as in obeying the voice of the Lord? To obey is better than sacrifice and to heed better than the fat of rams", 1 Samuel 15:22

After the disloyalty, I'm sure with all the combination of feelings of betrayal comes a landslide of questions. I've never counseled a married couple but I can only imagine what each of them might be asking themselves or the other.

Questions like, is he or she all to blame. Am I still handsome or pretty enough? What went stale in our marriage? How come I didn't see the signs? I should've never married him/her. I shouldn't have told my business to my girlfriend. She's probably the one who had the affair with the husband. When we continue to seek self gratification outside of the nest, bad things will always happen. Men tell their business too, I think they can just keep it better than women can.

In my earlier walk with God as a Christian, I backslid and fell out of fellowship with Christ. I used to live with my ex-fiancé but I had enough sense not to allow my female friends in my house, whether I was home or not. I didn't trust them or him. I did what I had to, to avoid the drama. I wasn't going to contribute to the cheating at home but that didn't keep him from going outside of the house to be unfaithful.

The marriage never took place and I had no business living with a man that was not my husband anyway, playing house. At that time I still confessed Jesus as Lord and Savior but I was not willing to live for Him. Therefore, He was my Savior but not Lord of my life. I felt like I deserved the hurt because I was living in sin. The things and people that I worshipped was my Lord. I was completely out of fellowship with God. I did some things while backslidden that I wouldn't tell anyone but God. I realized that the world is mad. It is crazy and the devil was having a field day, and he was getting plenty of help. Not just from his demonic friends, and his click of evil doers.

He was getting plenty of help from me. How was I helping him? Every time I would backbite and spread gossip I gave him fuel. Every time I lied and despitefully caused confusion, I gave him fuel. Every time I stole something, I gave him fuel. Every time I fornicated, I gave him fuel. He was feeding off of my evil ways. He kept coming back because I kept him fed. While I was feeding him, he was sucking the life out of me.

Lying was a blood clot. Stealing was a blood clot. Gossiping and backbiting were blood clots, fornication was a blood clot and the devil was just waiting for me to succumb. I had to starve him out. The Bible says to *"Submit to God, resist the devil and he will flee from you." James 4:7*. I hear this scripture quoted all the time, but people forget the part where it says **"Submit to God"**. First you have to submit to the power to get the power to resist the devil. The devil comes looking for in you, the very thing that represents him.

If lying is in you, he's coming because he's the father of lies. Whatever's in you that he identifies with is what he'll feed off of. Jesus said the enemy comes to me, but he finds none of him in me. What does God find when He comes to you? Just like the devil, God is looking for Himself in us as well. He's looking for the very thing that represents Him. Is His love in you? Then He's coming to see about you. Is His Word and truth in you? Then He's coming to perform Himself because He is His Word. Are His ways and His obedience in you? Then He's coming to use you for His glory.

When you are out of relationship with God, the longer you stay out there the worse you become. The longer you stay out there the harder it is for you to get back. The longer you stay out there the deeper the hole the devil will dig for you. The more he'll condemn you and make you feel like you're so far gone from God that even the Lord doesn't want you anymore. The devil is a liar. While out of relationship with God, every now and then I still felt the need to go to church. It was still rooted in me, but I was a true sinner. I broke every rule, every law and every vow in and out of the book. When there was nothing left, God threw the book at me.

The devil was having his way with me. I let him wine and dine me Monday through Saturday but God was my man on Sunday. I made love with the devil all week long and then gave God a little kiss on Sunday. God had kept me all week long and all I gave him was about thirty minutes of my time. Believers and non-believers alike, you know how we sometimes did and still do.

I made sure I missed devotional and the testimony part of the service. I would arrive just when I thought the preacher was ready to get up and preach. Then I would go to the bathroom and hope I ran into somebody so that I could hold a conversation with them passing the time. Then I would keep looking at my watch to see how fast time was moving.

Not to discredit the church or men of God in any way, but if you came from one of those old time Baptist churches where the preacher hooped and hollered instead of teaching and preaching, then you knew it was about to be over within the next five or ten minutes.

I went through the rest of the Sunday thinking that was pleasing to God just because I stepped foot in His house. Like I was really doing Him a favor; I was so deceived. God probably would have respected me more if I just stayed home. That's what happens when you backslide. Your spiritual eyes and ears become closed. Your spirit can no longer discern what is spiritually right or wrong. You become insensitive to the heart of God, misinterpreting His Word even to the point of using His Word to justify what you wrongly do, claiming that it is right. I took God's grace for granted and I was in a dangerous place.

Through it all, God remained faithful. Though I broke my vows to Him, He kept His to me. Though I broke my promises to Him, He kept His to me. Thank God for His grace and mercy. Thank God for His untiring forgiveness and thank God for His love. I apologized to God for my unfaithfulness. I had no peace in my spirit when I cheated on God. There was a void I was constantly trying to fill with all the wrong things.

I said "yes" to the world and "yes" to man. All I had to do was say "yes" to Jesus. I said "yes" to somethings when I really wanted to say "no". I denied who I was for the sake of pleasing people even when everything in me really didn't want to. I was out of fellowship with God and the devil had a power over me, using me as a puppet catering to everybody but Jesus. I became a wimp. The devil took my spiritual strength, my courage and my prayer life. I went from being saved to being and acting like a hypocrite with no anointing and no power. I knew the scriptures but I didn't have any power. The enemy wanted to keep me ignorant.

He had me thinking that just because I still knew a few things, I was alright. The devil is a liar. I wanted to come back to God but it seemed like everywhere I turned there was a roadblock. The enemy wasn't going to make it easy for me. He kept me lusting and not trusting the God I knew could deliver me. My heart was crying out. My heart was saying "God if you don't help me I don't know what I am going to do." My mind was screaming J-E-S-U-S help me! The enemy couldn't hear my thoughts. He can't read our minds but God can. He doesn't know what's in our hearts, but God does. I needed help and God was making a way. That wide road of destruction I was on was about to come to a close. This time God had set up a roadblock, right in the devils face. I was on my way back to God. Hallelujah!!!

I remember clearly the day I rededicated my life back to God. After the Lord threw the book at me, I came to my senses. I remember driving around the city that day. I felt like I was moving about in a trance like kind of state.

I felt like I was in a bubble. I tried to telephone several friends but they didn't answer. At that time I didn't own a cell phone. Pagers were the in thing. I carried a pager but that day no one would answer my page. Any other time it would be beeping or vibrating like crazy. I tried tracking friends down at all the hangouts and places where I knew I could find them, but they were not there, and then it seemed like the world just went quiet. I saw people moving their mouths but I couldn't hear a sound. I felt very strange as I came to the realization that God was trying to get my attention. He wasn't trying, He was getting it. I drove home and went into my bedroom.

There was such a heaviness on me, and I was soooooo tired. I fell on my knees at the foot of my bed and I cried like never before. If I wasn't wearing clothes to catch my tears, I would've been kneeling in a puddle of water. I prayed "Lord please forgive me, I surrender, make me whole like I used to be." I will never forget those words I prayed. I remembered what it was like to have the peace of God. I remembered what it felt like to be made whole. I remembered walking in the love of God. I remembered what it was like to cast all my cares upon Him.

Instantly, it was like the Lord scooped me up in His arms like a baby and every hurt, every pain, every burden and every disappointment I was carrying was lifted. All the shame from the things I had done was gone. My tears stopped flowing and I had such a peace, I knew the Lord had come to my rescue. I had been on a collision course. I was riding with a one-way ticket straight to hell. But GOD!!!!!!!!!

He loves me so much that He knew I couldn't help myself. He didn't send anyone to witness to me. He didn't allow me to experience a heart wrenching crisis. That day, He moved everything and everybody out of my reach. I had no one to run to, only Him. I had nowhere else to go but down on my knees. I still had enough left in me to know that if I called on the name of the Lord Jesus with a broken heart and a contrite spirit, that He would hear me, and receive me back. He said, "I'll never leave you or forsake you, I was always here." I was broken alright, shattered into so many pieces that the only one that could sweep me up was God.

Since that day I have never turned back. I believe that was my final call. Not from the mouth of man but from the Spirit of God drawing me back to Him. That was the day that I clocked in, in heaven and I'm not off until God calls me home. Then I'll have to clock in again. Oh yes, we will have to work. No, we won't be walking around heaven all day. What are we doing for the Lord in our daily lives here on earth? We're not walking around earth all day. How are we displaying His love toward one another? Who are we giving the good news of the Gospel of our Lord and Savior Jesus Christ?

The Bible tells us that *"For David had served God's purpose for his own generation, he fell asleep..." Acts 13:36"*. He had fulfilled his purpose on earth. When my work is finished on earth after I have served my generation, then I too will fall asleep and God will call me home. Hopefully it's no time soon. Until then I'm going to serve Him with all my heart, mind, soul and strength. He'll give me rest, but if I'm not working then I don't need any rest.

If all you do is lay around the house all day then you don't need any rest. If you're not working what are you doing?

Was it hard coming back to the Lord? It was indeed hard but I asked for forgiveness and I was forgiven. This time when I came back there was no going back. The devil had completely lost his opportunity to have my soul. He had more than one opportunity. In fact, he had too many but God had His hand on me and kept the devils hands off of me.

Psalms 32:1, "Blessed is he whose transgression are forgiven, whose sins are covered".

Proverbs 13:15, "Good understanding wins favor, but the way of the unfaithful is hard".

I John 1:9, "If we confess our sins He is faithful and just and will forgive us our sins and to purify us from all unrighteousness". That's good news.

We rebel against each other and sometimes we rebel against God. We get mad and just won't change until God fixes it or make it better. We can't make God do anything and then we act prideful, not wanting to apologize to God. God will let you pout for as long as you need to. You can throw a tantrum all you want to, but sooner or later you better humble yourself or He has a way of humbling you. Better you than Him.

It can be that way in a marriage; rebelling against each other. No one wants to make the first move. Each may feel that the other is the one who owes the apology.

Couples will go days without speaking to each other. Conversation is only for the sake of asking or answering a question. Sitting in the same room together is a no-no. Even coming straight home tends to get later and later. In bed, one or the other sleeps close to the edge making sure they don't feel so much as a toe from the other. The relationship is going into a danger zone. If too much time passes, that anger becomes bitterness. Given the situation, bitterness can turn to hatred and hatred can lead to unforgiveness.

When we carry a heart of unforgiveness, it can lead to thoughts of revenge and revenge ultimately leads to violence maybe even murder. God is a God of order, not confusion or chaos. That's the devil's job, and he does his job very well.

Just like in a marriage, we get an attitude with God. We don't want to speak to Him in the morning or in the evening. We miss a couple of

Sunday services thinking that's going to change how God sees us. God is not moved by our pity or our Oh woe is me party.

"......God opposes the proud and gives grace to the humble, 1 Peter 5:5".

Let us forgive even though it's hard to forget. God always forgave Israel and they broke His heart time after time after time. He can forgive and forget, though we can forgive but without His help we surely won't be able to forget.

In the book of Judges, in the beginning of several chapters, it's stated *"And Israel did evil in the sight of the Lord".* Every time they would cry out to God, He forgave them and rescued them out of bondage. The Bible says that the children of Israel were a "stiff necked people." They were a rebellious, disobedient, ungrateful, complaining people just like we are today. Seems like the more He did for them the more ungrateful they became. They were an unfaithful, adulterous people. God loved them so much and He still does. He was so fed up with their ways just like me, but His love exceeded His anger. At some point and time, God has to let you hurt. We're supposed to learn from our mistakes and our disobedience.

God is long suffering; the Bible doesn't say He suffers forever. Don't take His grace for granted. He's still a God of judgment.

8
The Divorce

A divorce of any kind is not good because there had to be something bad that led up to the divorce. In many cases two people just grew apart. It's even worse when children are involved. Why should divorce become part of the solution and who came up with irreconcilable differences?

Why can't couples work out their differences? Why can't they stay together for the sake of the children? When did they fall out of love with each other? How long has that secret affair been going on that you thought would never be found out? When does the wife find out about the other child or vice versa? Who gets hurt in a divorce? When, how, why, what, who and the list goes on. The questions never end.

Everyone gets hurt from the in-laws right down to the pets, unless the in-laws don't like you and vice versa. It can be devastating. Divorce is the ripping apart of the mind, soul, body and spirit. It is the splitting of one into two. How selfish can people be when it comes down to a divorce? Very.

I believe children suffer in a divorce more than anyone else. They tend to blame themselves. I believe children blame themselves because they see and hear arguments between parents that mention them but that are not about them. Adults can be very reckless around children when it comes to being discreet with their personal problems. I understand that some things cannot be avoided but sometimes they can. Divorcing each other is like divorcing God. The vow and the commitment are made to each other as well as God. You pledge your love for each other in the sight of God, until death due the two of you part. I do believe there are some marriages that are not joined by God. Some have married for the wrong reasons. In the end it's such a waste of time and money. Emotional pain and stress can get dragged into a new relationship overshadowed by a stigma from the last relationship.

The children of Israel tried God time and time again. They sinned and cried. Sinned and cried and each time God answered, forgave them and restored them. What kind of love does God have for Israel? Why did the children of Israel keep on sinning and God kept forgiving them? For the same reason we do it today. We all fall short and we have free will. Like David, Israel knew how to worship and pull on the heart strings of God.

They didn't just know how to worship, they knew how to cry out. They would make God so angry; and like a Father would do He fussed and chastised them.

Judges 2:12-14, "They forsook the LORD, the God of their fathers, who had brought them out of Egypt. They followed and worshiped various gods of the peoples around them. They provoked the LORD to anger. 12"Because they forsook him and served Baal and the Ashtoreths 13, "In his anger against Israel the LORD handed them over to raiders who plundered them. He sold them to their enemies all around, whom they were no longer able to resist."

They really tried God's patience but He couldn't avoid their cry. They knew how to confess from the heart and pull on the heartstrings of God. His soul was grieved at their cry.

THE DIVORCE | 69

Judges 10:10-16, "Then the Israelites cried out to the LORD, "We have sinned against you, forsaking our God and serving Baal."

11 The LORD replied, "When the Egyptians, the Amorites, the Ammonites, the Philistines,

12 the Sidonians, the Amalekites and the Maonites oppressed you and you cried to me for help, did I not save you from their hands?

13 But you have forsaken me and served other gods, so I will no longer save you.

14 Go and cry out to the gods you have chosen. Let them save you when you are in trouble!"

God was so fed up with them, though He fussed, like a Father would do He gave in to their tears. Again they cried out and again God came to their rescue.

15 But the Israelites said to the LORD, "We have sinned. Do with us whatever you think best, but please rescue us now."

16 Then they got rid of the foreign gods among them and served the LORD. And he could bear Israel's misery no longer.

After all the times God forgave Israel, they continued to sin in the eyes of the Lord. He was so upset with them that He called them backslidden. The children of Israel couldn't help themselves from going after other gods. Even God was fed up so He gave them a bill of divorce. It's bad when the Lord no longer wants you.

Jer. 3:8, 11-14 "And I saw, when for all the causes whereby backsliding Israel committed adultery I had put her away, and given her a bill of divorce; but her treacherous sister Judah feared not, but went and played the harlot also".

11, *"And the LORD said unto me, the backsliding Israel hath justified herself more than treacherous Judah".*

12, *"Go and proclaim these words toward the north, and say, Return, thou backsliding Israel, saith the LORD; and I will not cause mine anger to fall upon you: for I am merciful, saith the LORD, and I will not keep anger forever".*

13, *"Only acknowledge thine iniquity, that thou hast transgressed against the LORD thy God, and hast scattered thy ways to the strangers under every green tree, and ye have not obeyed my voice, saith the LORD".*

God is such a forgiving God. After all of that Israel again went whoring after other gods. Again He forgave them. It sounds like Israel took it as; as long as we repent and mean it God will keep on forgiving us. They didn't seem too concerned about the judgment part of it until they couldn't bare it anymore.

That's exactly how we treat God. We want to do whatever we want to do, when we want to do it until we're so wrapped up in it, it's about to destroy us. Then we run to Daddy and He responds. Here I am, come to Daddy. He takes us back because He's married to the backslider. He just waits for you to come back home.

14, *"Return, faithless people," declares the LORD, "for I am your husband. I will choose you, one from a town and two from a clan, and bring you to Zion*

So you see, as God waits He keeps the light on and the door unlocked just for you. Like a Father that cares would do.

9
Being Reconciled to God

After you have had a relationship with God and are no longer in fellowship with Him, a feeling of conviction should come over you every time you sin. The conviction of neglecting God should come over you. The weight of the conviction should feel like cinderblocks on your shoulders. You should feel bad but not condemned. Remember the devil condemns you and not God. Just as God forgives and restores with love, the devil condemns and make you feel unworthy of forgiveness and unworthy of God's love.

I believe that's one of the reasons why people commit suicide because they can't handle the guilt and the shame that the devil is making them feel like it is one hundred times worse than it really is. If God can have that kind of patience with the children of Israel, surely He can with you. It's not always as bad as it looks.

It's the devils job to make you think it's worse than it actually is. Why did I fall out of a relationship with God? It wasn't because God failed me, I failed Him. After I became a born again Christian, I didn't attend church on a regular basis like I should have to feed my spirit, my inner man. I needed the understanding, teaching and wisdom of the Bible to keep me grounded and rooted in my walk with Christ. Because I didn't attend a church gathering, I was starving my spirit of its spiritual food. I was spiritually dying and backslid as a result. I started doing what the old corrupt me used to do. If you starve your body of natural food, you'll eventually die from starvation. Just as it is in the spirit, so it is in the natural. When you become a born again Christian, you have to work at staying a born again Christian. A mechanic has to work on perfecting his skills as a mechanic. He just can't put new brakes on a car without the proper training. A chef has to work at perfecting his cooking skills. He can't prepare exquisite dishes without the proper training.

A Christian can't just confess with their mouth and believe in their heart that they are saved and after that never go to church or open their Bible. They have to make an effort to get to know God. More importantly, they should want to get to know more of God. They have to prove themselves; not to man but to God.

The Bible tells us to *"Do your best to present yourself to God as one approved, a workman who does not need to be ashamed and who correctly handles the word of truth.", 2 Timothy 2:15.* Why do we have to approve ourselves to God? We must be able to tell someone about His goodness according to the Bible.

We have to be able to clearly and truthfully present and represent Him. What about those who profess to be a Christian but there is no evidence of change and no effort made to grow? The Bible tells us that *"By their fruit you will recognize them..." Matthew 7:16.*

What are they producing? Is it like fruit unto Christ or is it like fruit unto that which is not of Christ? The Bible has an answer to whatever you need to know. You can rest assured that in spite of everything, God does love us unconditionally but He still hates the sin. When we fall out of touch with God, it changes our attitude. You'll cut someone short and be as nasty as a rattlesnake on your way to church. Before you realize what you've done, it's too late. How can you minister the love of Christ to that person next week when you just projected the hatred of the devil? You just told that same person last week that you were a Christian. In their eyes, you are a hypocrite. Unbelievers know how Christians are supposed to act. They watch you on your job and in your neighborhood, just waiting for you to cuss someone out, fight or fall into sin. Then the devil will use them to throw it up in your face, spread gossip about you, and insult the name of Jesus Christ.

That's why it's so important to pray. Prayer will give you staying power. Prayer will cause you to respond softly to a hyped up and crazy situation. Consistent lack of prayer will cause you to be weak and fall away from the faith. You have to have a prayer life if you're going to survive in your Christian walk. Prayer will fortify your mind. It will guard your heart and build a wall around your spirit. How we react to any given situation says something about what's going on in our spirit.

Temperance is so important. Self control will help you to respond and not to react harshly to a situation. What kind of prayers are you depositing in heaven to sustain you on earth? Whatever you deposit in heaven, you'll be able to make a withdrawal on earth and if you are praying, what are you praying? You have to read the Bible to be able to pray God's Word.

God is moved by His Words and not ours. The angels respond at His Word. It's His Word that will never return unto Him void, *Isaiah 55:11*. It is His Word that tears down, roots out, builds up and restores. It is His Word through prayer that is the hand that can go where we can't. There is no place God's Word can't reach. It is His Word that opens and close doors that no man can ever open or close. All you have to do is learn it so that you can speak it and put it in the atmosphere. You have to go to church to get understanding from the man of God concerning the things you don't understand in the Bible.

Salvation + the Bible + Prayer + Church = Life, Understanding, Power and Stability. Get the complete body, "God the Father", "God the Son", and "God the Holy Spirit." In order for your body to function properly, you can't just have an arm without a shoulder. You can't just have fingers without the hand and you can't just have a foot without the ankle. The one causes the other to move. They are all connected. Seek after what you don't know concerning God. Be humble enough to allow Him to reveal to you what your eyes have not seen or what your ears have yet to hear and that which has yet to enter into your heart. It can only be revealed to you by way of the Lord's Spirit, *I Corinthians 2:9-14*.

God loves you so much that He wants you to inquire of Him in all things. It doesn't matter what it is. There is nothing that can separate us from the love of God. He has an undying love for us. He's full of mercy and compassion. God's love is fully active in our lives every moment of the day, from the time He allows you to wake up in the morning, until you lie down to sleep at night, even if you don't acknowledge Him. It's not the alarm clock that wakes you up. It's the breath of life that God has allowed your body to keep using. It's the blood that He told to keep pumping through your heart and veins while you sleep. How can you not want to get to know this God?

In *Romans 8:35-37*, Paul asks the question, "Who shall separate us from the love of Christ? Shall trouble or hardship or persecution or famine or nakedness or danger or sword?"

36 *"As it is written: "For your sake we face death all day long; we are considered as sheep to be slaughtered."*

37 *"No, in all these things we are **more than conquerors** through him who loved us."*

With God's love for us, through Christ we can achieve anything. The devil is already defeated; therefore we can stand in the midst of adversity.

BEING RECONCILED TO GOD | 75

Paul reassures us with the answers to his own question and tells us we ought to be persuaded just as he was.

Romans 8:38-39 "For I am convinced that neither death nor life, neither angels nor demons, neither the present nor the future, nor any powers, Vs.39, neither height nor depth, nor anything else in all creation, will be able to separate us from the love of God that is in Christ Jesus our Lord."

Roman 8:35-37, says it all. We, who are in Christ Jesus, are the baddest created beings on the planet. God is married to those who are in Christ and we can always come back to Him. Jesus died for us so that not even death can separate us from God or His love. I can close the book right here.

"Therefore we are always confident and know that as long as we are at home in the body we are away from the Lord.", 2 Corinthians 5:6.

Life cannot separate us from His love; *"For to me to live is Christ, to die is gain.", Philippians 1:21*. Whatever you do, as long as you're in Christ, you're a winner.

Angels in heaven do as they are told. Like satan and the angels that followed him, rebellion against God is what got them kicked out of heaven. Rebellion against God will get us kept out of heaven too. If Angels had feelings and could speak to us about all that they have witnessed us doing wrong in the sight of God, I wonder what they would say. I wonder what they would say about all the chances God has given each and every one of us over and over again.

All the Angels in heaven know the awesomeness and love of God. They can't help but sing "Holy, Holy, Holy is the Lord God Almighty" because they keep seeing another awesome side to God that they haven't seen before.

Principalities and powers have no power over us. If we don't know who we are in Christ and use the authority that has been given to us, then we look weak in the eyes of the enemy and he will play us off base every time.

"You, dear children, are from God and have overcome them, because the one who is in you is greater than the one who is in the world.", 1 John 4:4.

Things present can't separate us because they will eventually perish, but the Word of God will stand. He's the same yesterday, today and forever. The things to come can't separate us because we look forward to the coming of Christ. He is our hope of Glory. We will be caught up in the air to finally meet and see Jesus.

Just like the ends of a rainbow cannot be traced, the width, length, depth and height of God's love for us cannot be measured. As the sky meets nothing but sky and beyond the sky into infinity, God simply cannot be measured. I understand how He can be the first, the last, the beginning and the end. He is the self existing one. He is the definition of all that was, is and is to come. No height beyond the heavens as we know it can separate us from His love. There is no depth beyond the fathoms of the unknown deep, where our minds can't even travel that can separate us from the love of God. There is nothing created in heaven or beneath heaven that can separate us from the love of God. It is finished, Hallelujah! These are true words of encouragement. Yes, God loves us in spite of anything, but He's not pleased with the sin in our lives.

He's not pleased with the things we practice as a lifestyle that destroys our soul, spirit and relationship with Him. If the children of Israel couldn't get away with sin, neither can we. If the angels in heaven couldn't get away with sin, surely we can't. Jesus is the way, He's the only way. Salvation is as vital to us as the blood that runs through our

BEING RECONCILED TO GOD | 77

veins. Prayer will keep you in the things of God. The Holy Spirit will empower you and give you staying power to stand when all hell is breaking loose around you. Get the complete package. Why would you want a gift in the form of an empty box? What good is the gift if you never open the gift? God the Father, God the Son, and God the Holy Spirit is the complete package. The gift is freely given to you.

You can go through life having been a complete, successful person, accomplishing every goal you ever set out to accomplish. But the day will come when you will have to stand before your Creator and face the music. Which song will you dance to? Will it be the "Well done my good and faithful servant" song or will it be the "Go away from me I never knew you song?" You will be without any excuse.

The book that is being kept on you in heaven is a constant witness to how you have lived your life on earth. You will have to give an account as a believer as well as an unbeliever. As an unbeliever, how do you explain to God that every time He knocked at your heart or every time He sent someone to witness to you with a tract, you didn't want to receive them or Him? How do you explain that every time someone invited you to come to church, you had an excuse? You never ran out of excuses and your excuses pushed you farther and farther away from the church and God.

Now picture this!!!! The last time someone invited you to visit their church was for this coming Sunday. Again you said "no" and you had another excuse. What you didn't know was that this was the day you were supposed to receive salvation. This was the day the sermon would locate where you were and your heart would be pricked. This was the day that you were supposed to come to the front of the church and receive salvation, while the Angels in heaven waited to rejoice over you, but again you said "no".

That Sunday evening you were involved in a freak hit and run car accident. Minutes later as you came to on the street, you got up and dusted yourself off. You watched as people began to gather and surround something that was badly mangled. You couldn't even make out what it was but you could identify the shoes and twisted jeans. You could also identify the tattoo on what appeared to be part of an arm lying close by. Though you couldn't see the face, you knew that it was you.

You had died from that fatal hit and run car accident. Panic and fear began to grip you. Immediately, all the mentioning of Jesus started to flood your mind. You started hearing all these voices of the people that tried to witness to you and you began to cry. Your life as you knew it was flashing before your eyes. You are fully aware of what's going on but no one can hear you or see you. Darkness starts closing in on you. There is no bright shining light beckoning you to come and there would be none. Your life on earth was over.

You now belong to the devil for all eternity, because you didn't believe and you didn't receive Jesus Christ in the pardoning of your sins. You had already belonged to satan, he was your God. You chose him over the Creator. He was your god if you were not serving God the Creator. You've lived according to your own standards and not God's. Hell is a real place and heaven is a real place. You wanted heaven but you didn't want God. The devil has to answer to the same God we all have to answer to. It was too late for you and satan was about to claim what was rightfully his, your soul.

But.................the good news is. If you are reading this book, then it's not too late! God is a forgiving God and right now, He's waiting for you. Do you really know where you will spend eternity if you ceased to breath in the next sixty seconds. Don't wait another minute. That's all it takes to change your life and it will determine where you will spend eternity. When you stand before God, you'll stand alone. Don't worry about what people say. If they call you a Jesus freak, be a Jesus freak. I'd rather be a freak for Jesus than to be a freak for man. Man can't speak for me when I stand before God, but Jesus can. I won't be ashamed of Him on earth, and He will not be ashamed to speak for me in heaven. Jesus freaks don't wait until night time to come out. We come out and stay out morning, afternoon and night!

Now let's bring the balance. Do you have to come to church to receive salvation? Absolutely not, God will meet you right where you are. But...........you come to church to hear the Word of God that your faith may increase, that your spirit will grow, mature in the things of God and that you gain a greater understanding of the Word of God.

"So then faith comes by hearing and hearing by the Word of God, Romans 10:17."

I like the way the Amplified version explains it.

"Faith comes by hearing what is told, and what is heard comes by the preaching of the message that came from the lips of Christ, the Messiah Himself, Romans 10:17."

You have to have enough faith to want to meet God, to believe that He is, and that He's a rewarder to them that diligently seek Him. *"Without faith it is impossible to please Him, Hebrews 11:6."* I challenge your faith. If you don't know God, I dare you to try Him. You have to try Him for yourself. It's a personal thing. Call upon Him with a broken heart and a contrite spirit. Humble yourself before the Lord and ask for His divine forgiveness.

To become a born again Christian you must receive Jesus as your Lord and Savior. Choose this day whom you will serve. Jesus had nails in His hands and nails in His feet but His mouth wasn't gagged. If it was He wouldn't have been able to say to the thief on the cross "today you'll be with me in paradise". He wouldn't have been able to say "Father forgive them, for they know not what they do." He would not have been able to say "It is finished".

Prayer of Salvation

If you have fallen out of fellowship with God and wish to be reconciled with Him or receive salvation for the first time, a simple heartfelt prayer of repentance and forgiveness will put you back in right standing with God. Please pray this prayer with an open heart.

Lord God, I acknowledge that I am a sinner saved by Your grace. I repent of my sins and confess that Jesus is Lord and Your Son. I believe that He died on the cross for me that I might be reconciled to You. Jesus, I ask You now to come into my heart and be Lord and Savior over my life. Wash me and cleanse me from all unrighteousness. I receive Your gift of Salvation. I ask this in the name of Jesus. Amen.

If you have prayed this prayer with a sincere heart of repentance, God has honored you. If you don't have a church home, quickly find one that teaches the raw uncut Word of God. Find a church home in a good Bible teaching church that will help you grow spiritually and learn of your destiny and purpose here on earth. God bless you and always remember:

John 3:16, "For God so loved the world that he gave his one Son and only Son, that whoever believes in him shall not perish, but have eternal life."

Please send all comments to godsfavor7@verizon.net

Other books written by the Author, Diane Wilson

To purchase a copy of "Silent Moments"
send a request to godsfavor7@verizon.net
or go to https://www.outskirts.com/silentmoments

A must read. Like an ocean breeze, "Silent Moments" will relax you and massage your mind. It will cause your imagination to take you to a place where you have never been before.

Coming soon by Diane Wilson

Silent Moments II
"A Collection of Inspirational Poems & True Stories"

Notes

Notes

Notes

Notes

Notes

Notes

Notes

Notes

Notes

Notes